P9-DGS-875

# THE CAMBRIDGE BIBLE COMMENTARY

NEW ENGLISH BIBLE

GENERAL EDITORS

## P. R. ACKROYD, A. R. C. LEANEY,
## J. W. PACKER

# UNDERSTANDING THE OLD TESTAMENT

# UNDERSTANDING
# THE OLD TESTAMENT

### EDITED BY
## O. JESSIE LACE

*Formerly Senior Lecturer and Tutor*
*William Temple College, Rugby*

### CAMBRIDGE
## AT THE UNIVERSITY PRESS
### 1972

Published by the Syndics of the Cambridge University Press
Bentley House, 200 Euston Road, London NW1 2DB
American Branch: 32 East 57th Street, New York, N.Y.10022

Library of Congress Catalogue Card Number: 75–178282

ISBNS:
0 521 08415 6 hard covers
0 521 09691 x paperback

Printed in Great Britain
at the University Printing House, Cambridge
(Brooke Crutchley, University Printer)

# GENERAL EDITORS' PREFACE

The aim of this series is to provide commentaries and other books about the Bible, based on the text of the New English Bible, and in these various volumes to make available to the general reader the results of modern scholarship. Teachers and young people have been especially kept in mind. The commentators have been asked to assume no specialized theological knowledge, and no knowledge of Greek or Hebrew. Bare references to other literature and multiple references to other parts of the Bible have been avoided. Actual quotations have been given as often as possible.

The completion of the New Testament part of the series in 1967 provides a basis upon which the production of the much larger Old Testament and Apocrypha series can be undertaken. The welcome accorded to the series has been an encouragement to the editors to follow the same general pattern, and an attempt has been made to take account of criticisms which have been offered.

The series is accompanied by three volumes of a more general character, designed to provide in somewhat greater detail the background information which is needed for the study of the books of the Old Testament and which can only be sketched in very brief form in the separate commentary volumes. This one, *Understanding the Old Testament*, sets out to provide the larger historical and archaeological background, to say something about the life and thought of the people of the Old Testament, and to answer the question 'Why should we study the Old Testament?'. Its companion, *The Making of the Old Testament*, is concerned with the formation of the books of the Old Testament and Apocrypha in the context of the ancient Near Eastern world, and with the ways in which these books have come down to us in the life of the Jewish and Christian communities. The third volume, *Old Testament Illustrations*, contains maps, diagrams and photographs with an explanatory text. These three volumes are designed to provide material helpful to the understanding of the individual books and their commentaries, but they are also prepared so as to be of use quite independently.

P. R. A.
A. R. C. L.
J. W. P.

# CONTENTS

### 3   THE HISTORY OF RELIGION IN ISRAEL
#### *By O. Jessie Lace*

# CONTENTS

# ILLUSTRATIONS

# I

## THE OLD TESTAMENT AND APOCRYPHA

The New English Bible is divided into three sections, the Old Testament, the Apocrypha and the New Testament. Although in some other Bible translations the Apocrypha is omitted or comes at the end, it is in many ways closely related to the Old Testament, and that is why Old Testament and Apocrypha are studied together in this series. Of the sections the Old Testament is by far the largest, and it does in fact consist of three distinct parts, the Law, the Prophets and the Writings, so we have really four sections to study. Three of the four have come to be regarded as one whole without the Apocrypha and the reasons for this are part of a long story. The details of that story may be found in *The Making of the Old Testament*, one of the other books in this series.

The division of the Old Testament into three sections does not correspond to the order in which the individual books occur in the English Bible. It does correspond to the order of the Hebrew Bible and the three main stages of its growth. The first section is known in English as the Law (Genesis, Exodus, Leviticus, Numbers, Deuteronomy), but 'Law' is not an adequate translation of the Hebrew word 'Torah'. Torah cannot really be translated by one word; 'teaching' is sometimes used and this is satisfactory provided it is taken to mean teaching about every conceivable thing – God and man, life and death, human relations of every kind and standards of behaviour

I

both individual and corporate. The second section, Prophets, is sub-divided into Former (Joshua, Judges, 1 and 2 Samuel, 1 and 2 Kings) and Latter (Isaiah, Jeremiah, Ezekiel and The Twelve). This second section includes books which have often been described as 'historical', and it is a fact that there is a great deal of narrative in them, but so there is in Exodus. So it seems that the old Hebrew descriptions were concentrating on characteristics which are not the same as the ones which enable us to use labels like 'history', 'poetry', 'laws' and 'prophecy'. The third section, Writings (Psalms, Job, Proverbs, Ecclesiastes, Song of Songs, Ruth, Lamentations, Esther, Daniel, Ezra, Nehemiah, 1 and 2 Chronicles), does not seem to carry any implication in its title. Its various units are in different order in different Bible manuscripts and they are only linked together by the fact that at about the end of the first century of the Christian era they were judged by certain religious leaders to carry religious authority. The Torah had carried authority at least since about 400 B.C. and the Prophets since 200 B.C. or thereabouts.

When the list of the Writings was agreed there were also in use a number of other books of similar kinds; some of these are in the Apocrypha (1 and 2 Esdras, Tobit, Judith, The Rest of Esther, The Wisdom of Solomon, Ecclesiasticus, Baruch, A Letter of Jeremiah, More of the Book of Daniel, The Prayer of Manasseh, 1 and 2 Maccabees) and some of them were used alongside other religious books in one or other of the many countries in which there were well-established Jewish communities at the beginning of the Christian era. Yet other books besides those included in the Apocrypha are still found from time to time and add to our knowledge of the past, sometimes very considerably. A great deal of manuscript material has been found in the area around the Dead Sea since the first scrolls were found there accidentally, in 1947.

The Jewish community, which includes many shades of opinion, still places very high value on the Old Testament, while Christians, too, hold much of it to be in some sense binding. Yet a great deal of it seems very remote from the twentieth century in most parts of the world. We may applaud the injunction 'You must love the LORD your God...' (Deut. 6: 5) and dismiss as of secondary importance the details of ancient religious ceremonies (Lev. 16). We may be intrigued to compare 'Do not move your neighbour's boundary stone' (Deut. 19: 14) and 'A curse upon him who moves his neighbour's boundary stone' (Deut. 27: 17). This comparison illustrates how commands and penalties have developed. Cheating about entitlement to land is a serious offence everywhere, not necessarily for abstract moral reasons but because the supply of food depends on farming the land. So the boundary stone is an important factor in relationships; custom develops, the prohibition follows and frequently the strong condemnation of those who fail to conform. There may perhaps be a stage when the custom is detached from its origins and some will say that the custom is something which has been ordained by God. Then the exhortations and the prohibitions and the penalties are also all believed to be God's word.

This stage causes a number of profound changes in habits and customs which will be analysed in greater detail later in this book. Some men and women are happy to believe that God, whom they worship and to whom they willingly submit, has laid down in advance the details of the ways in which human beings are to

3

behave. Others have no such belief in God and understand habits and customs as being part of an inherited pattern, accumulated and modified in the past and having to be again modified in the present. Others again are in a more complex position: they believe that this process of growth stems from experience and does not depend upon arbitrary principles laid down in the beginning. At the same time they believe in God and that his way of working is to leave man free to discover for himself what ways of behaving are most conformable to the nature and purposes of human life. This is not to claim that what seems to work best is necessarily what God intends: it is only to suggest that through this kind of process those who believe in God come to have convictions about what it is that God does intend. Not even depth of conviction is guarantee of harmony with what God wills—there is no guarantee. But long stretches of the story of religion are about the search for such a guarantee and the obstinate hope of finding it.

In the modern world we know much more about each other even than was possible a hundred years ago. So it ought not to be so difficult for us to understand that other people in other times as well as in other places have had convictions about right and wrong which they held passionately and which may be quite different from ours. These beliefs and convictions can be studied in their own right, whether or not we hold them now ourselves, and the study of them is a necessary part of any attempt to understand their modern successors. Modern patterns of belief may be direct successors, or they may be systems offered as alternatives, maybe as part of a general revolt against traditional patterns. Statesmen and politicians are well advised to study the background and reasons for their own views and those of their opponents; all reasonable citizens have as part of their responsibility to try to understand themselves and those who differ from them.

The Old Testament still carries supreme authority for Jews: for Christians, too, it is part of authoritative scripture. As time goes on, this calls for justification and explanation, especially if the place of religion in human life is being challenged. The fact that something is described as 'old' is not sufficient reason for discarding it or disregarding it. But with new discoveries and new developments a new generation may question the value of long-cherished customs and may swing over to a position where the word 'new' carries an implication of superiority. If a conflict develops it will not be very long before personal tastes and preferences come in and the result will depend on whether individual views can be reconciled or not. It was taken for granted earlier on that everybody would agree that Leviticus 16 with its ceremonial details is less relevant than parts of Deuteronomy where religious principles are laid down, but perhaps this is not true. Personal opinion or taste is a very powerful criterion. It may be a genuinely individual matter or it may work through fashion, which in its turn varies as time goes on. So it is that for some people, at some times, 'old-fashioned' will be a term of commendation. In other circumstances it can indicate patronage or even contempt.

The second half of the twentieth century is often described as a period of rapid social change. The big and obvious changes brought about by technological development are affecting human life in so many ways so quickly that the day-to-day living of human beings is changed too. The result of this is that some of the old conventions and rules are of no use any more. Rules of the road made when vehicles were drawn by horses are just useless for modern traffic on modern roads. Habits and customs change too. Family relationships can be quite deeply influenced by changes in patterns of housing and new methods of transport; deliberate decisions have to be made about what to do in new situations. So social customs change, sometimes slowly, sometimes quite fast, sometimes by sheer force of circumstances, sometimes by conscious, planned, human decision. The generations which are used to old patterns may resent and criticize the new, but they may welcome the new if they judge that here are new possibilities for better relationships and fuller human living. The young may take the new for granted and despise the old, but they may prefer to cling to the old if it seems to offer greater security and to make fewer demands upon them.

We are all involved in changing and being changed; we all make judgements about the old and the new, and our judgements do not always agree. Differences are not just differences of age but of education and upbringing and frequently of religion. Even in a society where everyone has the same religion there can be differences of view. In a society where different religions are represented and some people adhere to none there will be many deep differences. Many customs and laws are closely tied up with religious beliefs, which often means that some people regard them as unchangeable. This can cause serious crisis and some people will withdraw from change while others will repudiate the authority which is forbidding the change. Nevertheless, new customs and new ideas are continually being added to the accumulation which has been inherited. While this goes on, some new ideas are rejected, not necessarily for well-thought-out reasons but just because they are not acceptable to the majority or to some specialized group. Some of these may be kept alive by minority groups and come to general notice again later on.

Every society, and every individual within it, inherits a long history of experience and judgement and decision, and most of it without question. Many societies have their historians who study and analyse the past and show how it explains the present. When historians tell us about the past they are not simply telling us what happened long ago. They are telling us what they judge to be important and the records they study have already been shaped by the work of earlier historians who have passed on what *they* judged to be important. So what we learn from the study of written history is what our predecessors have thought was important, though some of it may seem very unimportant to us. If we happen to be interested in social conditions and can only find out about wars and disputes between nations this can be very frustrating and we may be driven to think that our predecessors were more interested in national prestige than in the quality of life of people in general. We may be right about this, and if so we have identified a change of emphasis in ourselves and our contemporaries. Nowadays history is understood in a very wide sense, and professional historians are discussing how history can be written and taught so as to give people as wide an understanding as possible. Nothing, however, can alter the fact that writers write about what is judged to be, or to have been, important, and readers must constantly remind themselves of this.

Religion is one of the most powerful factors in human

affairs – perhaps the most powerful of all. Certainly this has been true in the past, though many would question whether it is still so. Many nowadays who recognize the power of religious ideas believe that religion is an adverse influence and would like to free mankind from it. In this situation the many millions of adherents of the great religions of the world have to prepare themselves to enter into debate. It is not sufficient, and it is certainly not convincing to opponents, just to stand in defence of traditional positions and refuse to discuss them. If discussion is to be fruitful, however, it must be well informed and the purpose of this book is to present some of the material necessary for an adequate understanding of the Old Testament.

One result of this should be to see more clearly the characteristics of the religion which the Old Testament preserves. It is not possible to do this by simply reading the book, as many have found to their confusion and distress. There are a number of reasons for this. One is because of the complicated story which lies behind the text that we read, the story that is told in *The Making of the Old Testament*. Another is because of the great variety of ideas and beliefs which are still included within the Old Testament. Some of these ideas diverge sharply from one another and even when one has finally won the day others may still survive, if only in the way that a story is told and what it implies. The variety is present also because of the many different ways that men have gone about interpreting their life and experience and relating it to beliefs about the supernatural. The Old Testament and Apocrypha are fascinating to study because this rich variety is found within them.

There is a powerful common characteristic as well – the

deep concern of the writers and editors that their readers, or rather their hearers, for very few could read in those days, should know about the important happenings of the past. They claim to tell what has been important and sometimes why, what has been right and wrong and why, what is true and false and why. How do they know? Are they right? They have no doubts about their rightness or about the authority upon which they depend. Nevertheless they do not always agree. Can we come to any decision about these beliefs? Evidently they must be studied as carefully as possible and that is what we are setting out to do.

We have two main sources of information, the Old Testament and Apocrypha themselves and our knowledge of the ancient world of the Near East, much of which has been derived from the finds of archaeologists. From the interpretation of archaeological material we learn about history in the wide sense, about daily life and about political and economic affairs. This is a most valuable contribution to the study of the old texts because it provides clues about the meanings of words and episodes and customs which in the past have not been understood or have been misunderstood. Many of the moral judgements made in the Old Testament relate to social conditions and patterns which are taken for granted. Some understanding of this background will make it more likely that we shall understand what points were really being made.

We are fortunate to be trying to understand the Old Testament at a time when the studies of language and manuscripts, as well as beliefs and customs, are sufficiently advanced for us to be taking a new overall view. Strong evidence that this is so is provided by the readiness of a great number of scholars to spend time on the massive task of translating into English all over again from the old texts. The first translation of the whole Bible into English was made in the fourteenth century, and since then there have been other versions and many revisions, particularly in the nineteenth and twentieth centuries. But now we have a new translation, the New English Bible, and it is in relation to this translation that the volumes in the Cambridge Bible Commentary are being produced. This title, 'The New English Bible', has been challenged – how can the Bible be new? There is a sense, of course, in which it can never be new, or old either; its quality of agelessness is one of its most astonishing characteristics. The important thing is to keep renewing the way in which it is made available for people to read and study. If it cannot be renewed to keep pace with all kinds of other new understandings, then the claims made for it must fall to the ground; it cannot be alive after all. In the main chapters of this book the results of some of the studies which have contributed to the new situation will be set out so as to help readers of the new translation to understand it more readily.

# 2

# THE CONTEXT OF THE OLD TESTAMENT

## THE GEOGRAPHICAL SETTING

The geography of the Old Testament must be treated in two different ways: we need a fairly detailed picture of the country we call Palestine, but the rest of the world known to the Old Testament may be sketched in broader outline.

Palestine itself is the piece of territory which forms the southern part of the eastern seaboard of the Mediterranean; and the world with which the Old Testament concerned itself consisted of its close neighbours, among which the names of at least two – Syria and Arabia – are in use today. Somewhat further away there were two great river-valley centres, Egypt and Mesopotamia, whose numerical, economic and cultural superiority always tended to overshadow the history and attainments of Palestine – the 'poor relation' which both joined and separated them. Palestine had links with other countries too, which will be mentioned later, but they were less frequent.

Although Palestine is quite easy to locate, it is not so easy to draw its exact boundaries. Except for the obvious western limit, which is the seacoast, there is no other natural feature sufficiently dominant to form a permanent frontier, whether to the north, east or south. Political boundaries have often altered, ever since the beginning of biblical times, and maybe always will. This does not

1. Palestine

mean that noticeable, even remarkable, natural features do not occur; they do, but they are a divisive rather than a uniting factor. The most remarkable feature of Palestine is undoubtedly the deep rift valley along which three rivers flow. It starts right up north near the Turkish border as the bed of the river Orontes; it continues south between the Lebanon and Anti-Lebanon mountains and, when the river Litany (Leontes) in its turn breaks out to

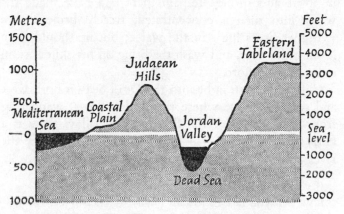

Fig. 2. East–West cross-section of Palestine

the sea, to the west above Tyre, finally the Jordan river takes its place, flowing from the slopes of mount Hermon, first through marshy lake Huleh (now drained), then through lake Tiberias (the Sea of Galilee) and ending in the Dead Sea. The remarkable thing is that the surface of the Dead Sea is the lowest place on the face of the globe – 1,285 feet below mean sea-level (its bed lies 1,300 feet lower still). Even lake Tiberias is 695 feet below sea level. The level of the rift valley bottom gradually rises on its course south from the Dead Sea before dropping again to sea-level at Aqaba at the north-east extension of the Red Sea. The reason why this whole valley does not fill up and become a long lake flowing out into the sea is that the evaporation from the surface of the Dead Sea is sufficient to balance the amount of water flowing into it. And that is the reason why this sea is 'dead'; it is so salty that no fish can live in it. The sun draws up only pure water vapour so that all the chemicals which have been flowing into the Dead Sea over the centuries in rivers and springs remain there and have made the water into such a concentrated, treacly brine that a swimmer floats high in the water; but he should keep it out of his eyes, and wash the brine off his skin as soon as he comes ashore.

Cliffs plunge straight into the Dead Sea on both west and east sides, but where the Jordan flows, wandering from side to side of the floor of the valley, there is a fairly narrow groove (in Arabic, the *Zor*), worn by the river and its floods and choked with undergrowth.

> If you fall headlong in easy country,
> how will you fare in Jordan's dense thickets? (Jer. 12: 5)

The rift valley floor (in Arabic, the *Ghor*) is therefore on a higher level and depends for water, and so fertility, on streams from the mountains which form the steep sides of the rift valley. Since these are usually higher on the east side and also face the moisture-laden winds from the Mediterranean, the east bank is much better watered. But even so there are sterile, salty stretches near the edge of the *Zor*.

Four main tributaries run into the rift valley from the east. The Zered runs into the south end of the Dead Sea; the Arnon halfway along its east side; the Jabbok north of the Dead Sea, about one-third of the distance towards lake Tiberias; and, lastly, the Yarmuk just south of lake Tiberias. These rivers get their waters from the well-watered and fertile plateau immediately east of the Jordan valley. Further east the rainfall tails off rapidly and the ground becomes wilderness and desert, and takes us out of Palestine into Syria, Iraq and Arabia.

So much for the eastern side of Jordan. If we climb to the top of the steeper slope on the west of the Jordan valley, in the distance, about 30 miles away, we may catch a glint of the Mediterranean sea.

The coastline runs roughly north to south, as do most of the other natural features of the land, though some run at right angles, and others at roughly 45 degrees, to the main axis. The shore is almost entirely a gently sloping, sandy beach; consequently natural harbours are very few, in fact there are only two worth noting. About halfway up the coast is the little port of Joppa (modern Jaffa), which is really only a small cove where a ridge of rock runs out into the sea. Then, some 60 miles further north, the port of Acco developed where a small tongue of land afforded a little shelter to shipping in the northern corner of the wide, shallow bay which extends north from mount Carmel. The large present-day port of Haifa at the southern end of this bay, and immediately under the slopes of mount Carmel, is a modern development artificially created by building a huge breakwater offshore. One other artificial harbour once existed, though not in Old Testament times; this was Caesarea, built by king Herod. He managed to raise a protective breakwater on some convenient reefs, and developed the city so that it became in time the capital of the Roman province. The absence of natural harbours is one reason why, even when their territory extended to the coast, the Israelites never developed as sailors, unlike the inhabitants of Phoenicia, further north, where there is a much more indented coastline.

Inland from the coast is a fairly flat plain of clay or loess, some 25 miles wide in the south at Gaza but narrowing to almost nothing below the tip of mount Carmel. The coastal plain is very fertile, especially if irrigation is used to counteract the effects of the low rainfall in the south.

Further inland than the coastal plain, and marked off from it by a geological fault, there is a north-to-south band of moderately hilly country often broken by fairly deep, east-to-west valleys or wadis; this is the area known in the Old Testament as the Shephelah, literally the Lowland and so called even though it may rise to at least 1,000 feet. But this is much lower than the high, narrow backbone which comes next, before the sudden plunge down into the Jordan valley.

This central backbone is a high ridge mainly above the two-thousand-foot contour-line. It runs north to south without significant interruption except at one point where part of it seems to have been pushed aside like a door to form a south-east-to-north-west spur that runs into the Mediterranean Sea and is called mount Carmel. In the doorway thus opened the valley of Jezreel runs through from the Jordan north-westwards, broadening out over the watershed, into the plain which is drained by the river Kishon into the Haifa bay: this plain is commonly known by its later name of Esdraelon. As it keeps below 250 feet it provides the lowest route from the coast to the Jordan valley, which is why the railway line to Damascus was built along it. Another important east-to-west crossing passes between the peaks of mount

Ebal and mount Gerizim, a little further south. But, though one or two other valleys lead up from the west to the central ridge, there are no other easy descents into the Jordan valley – the least difficult is from a little north of Jerusalem to Jericho. Where the central ridge loses height, south of Hebron, and merges into the semi-desert Negeb, the water-supply was too precarious to make a west-to-east route, via Beersheba for example, really practical, though it was used, and at various times this arid area has supported small centres of population, from necessity expert in water-conservation.

## Climate and crops

Having tried in this way to outline the main geographical features of Palestine we must now look at the climate and natural products of the land. Rainfall is in four main bands. The Lebanon and Anti-Lebanon (Hermon) mountains receive as much as 60 inches per annum (including the winter snows) on account of their great altitude. Next come the Carmel spur and the rest of the central highlands and the mountains of Transjordan, which receive about 25 or 30 inches. All the westward-facing area of Palestine, with Galilee and parts of Transjordan, may expect quite a bit of seasonal rain, from 15 to 25 inches; but once south of a line through Hebron and once over the edge into the Jordan valley or east of the Transjordan slopes, rainfall drops rapidly from 10 inches down to nothing. Rainfall varies in total from year to year very considerably, and the effect of a dry year can be as disastrous as the extra rain of a wet year can be beneficial. In southern Palestine especially the boundary between cultivated land and desert is rarely fixed and may shift tens or even scores of miles. The effect of drought is described in 1 Kings 17: 7 and contrasts sharply with the idealized picture in Isaiah 35: 1–2, 6–7. Rain is never expected between the beginning of May and the latter part of September; it falls mostly between October (the former or early rains) and March (the latter rains). Ploughing cannot start until the first rains have softened the soil, and grain will not mature properly without the latter rains. What keeps crops growing during the dry summer months, without irrigation, is the moisture which condenses as dew and the blankets of wet mist, both of which occur regularly over large areas of Palestine.

The natural vegetation of Palestine depends mainly on rainfall, dew and mist, though it must be remembered that there is also a considerable range of temperature. Coldest (and wettest) are the heights of Lebanon and mount Hermon, where some snow remains even in summer, and this is where the famous evergreen cedars once grew in profusion. In contrast, the Jordan valley is always warm even in winter and stiflingly hot in summer; in its natural state it is too dry to grow any vegetation of note, but when watered by natural springs, or artificially, it would grow date palms, as at Jericho; the waters of the local springs nowadays ensure heavy crops of bananas there. Along the banks of the river Jordan itself there still grows a thick jungle-like undergrowth of thorn and tamarisk.

Between these climatic extremes the better-watered highlands with their warm days and cool nights seem in Old Testament times to have been fairly thickly forested with such trees as oaks, pines, cypresses, figs, pomegranates and olives. The latter would of course also grow on the lower slopes, where the climate is more humid.

Vines were freely grown on suitable sites, especially round Hebron.

Without irrigation the drier parts would obviously produce only scrub and scanty pasture. These would feed wandering flocks of sheep and goats, tended then as now by fully or semi-nomadic herdsmen. The Canaanites seem to have kept a lot of pigs. Cattle needed richer pastures – like those of Bashan east of lake Tiberias. Horses were only for royalty or the nobility and for use in wars; when not in use they probably spent most of their time in stables.

The Israelites apparently did not make much use of the camel – the animal of the real desert-dweller – but everyone seems to have had his donkey either for carrying loads or for riding. Mules, though actually forbidden to the Israelites by the law against hybrids (Lev. 19: 19), do seem to have been used from quite early times for riding (2 Sam. 13: 29).

The agricultural crops grown by the Israelites included several sorts of grain, especially wheat and barley, and beans and lentils. These – either as bread or as stew – formed the basic food of the people, eked out by vegetables such as onions, cucumbers, melons, radishes, garlic and various herbs; possibly also lettuce and various nuts and fruits.

The lakes and perennial streams, like the sea itself, provided many varieties of fish; piles of empty shells show that shellfish were eaten. Along the Phoenician coast too were found the murex shellfish which yielded the purple dye which was so noteworthy that it gave its name to the people who traded in it (Greek *phoinos*, purple). Meat was a luxury, though the huntsman would undoubtedly try for wild boar, deer and antelope as well as for smaller game; at the same time he would have to be on his guard against such competitors as lions, leopards, bears and wolves, now no longer met with in Palestine. The number of words in the Old Testament for 'snare' and 'net' shows that scarcely a bird was safe from the fowler. The annual migratory flights of birds such as quails were no doubt useful seasonal sources of food, but other species such as partridges and pigeons might be caught at any time of the year, and even sparrows. At least by the Persian period, poultry as well as pigeons, and possibly geese, were kept for food; their eggs would also be a useful addition to the diet. So was the milk of domestic cattle, goats and sheep, which was usually preserved from going sour by turning it into a form of yoghurt (curds, Arabic *leben*) or butter.

Probably the only major change in animal population since Old Testament times has been the virtual extermination of all large beasts of prey, but the severe erosion which has followed the constant destruction of all forests must also have reduced the numbers of most other wild animals.

It is sometimes maintained that the climate of Palestine too has changed over the centuries; but, although there are apparently alternating cycles of dry and wetter seasons, there is little evidence of any permanent alteration having taken place within historical times.

### Israel's neighbours

Due east of Palestine there is desert – the northern continuation of the great Arabian desert – which cannot support any considerable population. Israel's neighbours on this side therefore were small groups of tribes very similar in many respects to herself in language and custom, the chief of whom were known as Edom, Moab and Ammon. The first-named had the area mostly south and south-east of the Dead Sea; Moab bordered the Dead Sea on the east and Ammon stretched from there northwards until it met some of the minor Aramaean states between Palestine proper and Damascus, the capital city of Aram, the country we know as Syria. Syria seems to have been more a political entity than a geographical one. Geographically it is a continuation of Palestine, with no well-marked frontier, but it was peopled by Aramaeans whose small kingdoms seem to have formed some sort of federation under the overlordship of the king of Damascus. They were great traders and carried their language, Aramaic, into Asia Minor and even as far as China. In later years it became an official diplomatic language of the Persian empire and even threatened the existence of the Hebrew language spoken by the Israelites. Aramaic and Hebrew are closely related, but differ considerably from one another, both in form and structure.

It is interesting to realize that when the Israelites entered Canaan, as the country was then called, they probably spoke an Aramaean dialect, but exchanged it for Hebrew – the language of Canaan – which they found being spoken there as in Moab and indeed with some differences up the west coast in Phoenicia (modern Lebanon).

One other, quite different, language spoken in Palestine was that of the Philistines, whose territory was an integral part of Palestine geographically and as such has already been described. Basically it stretched from the sea coast, as far north as Carmel, inland to the frontier with the Israelites. It seems that the Israelites and the Philistines invaded Palestine about the same time. For a time it seemed that the Philistines would gain the upper hand; since Roman times their name, in the form 'Palestine', has been used for the land. But it was the Israelites who became its masters and, after the days of David, only very few references to anything distinctively Philistine are found in the Bible, though a number of Philistine cities retained at least semi-independent status and are mentioned in Assyrian records. Only a few words of the Philistine language are known and these, as might be expected, confirm a link with the Aegean islands and Asia Minor. (The word 'prince', as in 1 Sam. 5: 8, translates *seren*, which is probably the same as the Greek *tyrannos*.) How long this language continued to be spoken in Philistia is doubtful, but some believe it was the 'language of Ashdod' spoken by some semi-Jews in Nehemiah's time (Neh. 13: 24).

## (a) *Egypt*

If we look further afield than these very confused and confusing small states of Palestine, we begin to find large states whose existence was very well known to the Israelites – indeed at least some of the Israelites spent years as second-class citizens in two of them. The first is Egypt, the valley of the river Nile which runs into the Mediterranean Sea at the north-east corner of Africa, on a course parallel to the Red Sea and the gulf of Suez.

This long, narrow land is bordered by high desert plateaux on each side, and the extraordinary fertility of its soil is due to the fresh mud spread over the face of the land by the flooding of the Nile, which begins in June or July, reaches its peak in October and ends in January. Rain is unusual in Egypt itself; the flooding is

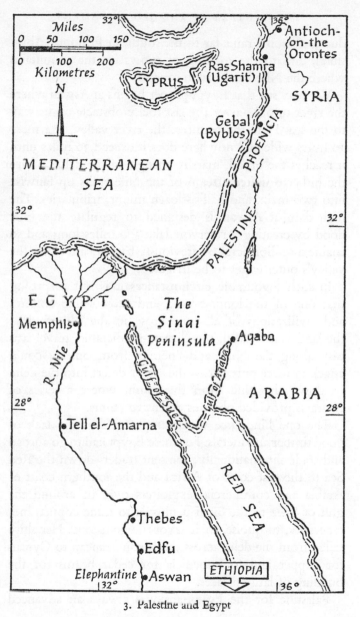

3. Palestine and Egypt

23

due to seasonal rains far to the south, in Ethiopia (Abyssinia), and to the melting of snows on the mountains where the Nile has its twin sources.

We may say that Egypt proper begins at Aswan where the river tumbles over the last rocky obstacle on its way to the sea. Here the country, the river valley, is a mere 10 miles wide and nowhere does it exceed 30 miles until it reaches the broad, marshy triangle of the delta, where the hitherto united stream of the Nile splits up fanwise into two main, and half-a-dozen minor, tributaries. The high dam at Aswan is designed to regulate the Nile flood by creating a reservoir lake 300 miles long and so enable 2 million acres of previously barren land along the valley's outer edges to be irrigated.

In such favourable circumstances it is not surprising that one of the longest-lived and most stable empires and civilizations of all time arose in the Nile valley: the land was fruitful, the climate predictable, travel was easy along the Nile, and enemies from outside could attack in force only across the sea or desert into the delta or down the Nile from the south, where a series of cataracts provided obvious defensive points.

The one hindrance to development was the lack of good timber and metals. For these Egypt had to go abroad and trade internationally; she sent traders down the Red Sea to the east coast of Africa and the southern coast of Arabia and commercial exploiters over or around the gulf of Suez to the Sinai peninsula to mine copper and, especially, turquoise, their favourite gemstone. Her ships sailed from the delta across the Mediterranean to Cyprus for copper and to Phoenicia for cedar beams for the building of large palaces.

Palestine for the Egyptians was always an advanced

frontier zone, a useful training-ground for her armies and a source of revenue; Egypt for the Hebrews was a refuge in time of famine, the seat of advanced knowledge, a source of possible military support against any other great power who might threaten her peace, and a demanding and inconsiderate taskmaster.

Of lands beyond Egypt the Hebrews probably had only vague notions, though the land of Cush (Nubia), the stretch of Nile valley south of Egypt proper, was known to them as a land on the fringe of civilization.

## (b) *Mesopotamia*

Mesopotamia lies due east of Palestine, beyond the virtually impassable Arabian desert. To get to it from Palestine it is necessary to travel north and then east and pass through Damascus to the east of the Lebanon and Anti-Lebanon ranges where a well-known trade-route led north of the desert via Tadmor (Greek Palmyra) into the valley of the Euphrates river. A still easier route lay farther north still, through Aleppo, which avoided the Syro-Arabian desert altogether and reached the Euphrates before the river had turned from its north-to-south flow to its south-east course. The Euphrates is the longer of the two rivers which together enclose the land known today as Iraq but previously by its Greek name Mesopotamia, 'Between the Rivers'. The other river is the Tigris. Both rise in the mountains of Asia Minor and flow roughly parallel with one another, finally uniting before reaching the Persian gulf; some say that there was a time when the two rivers had separate mouths.

Like the Nile, these two rivers bring down a tremendous amount of sediment, especially during the peak flow during April and May, caused by the melting of

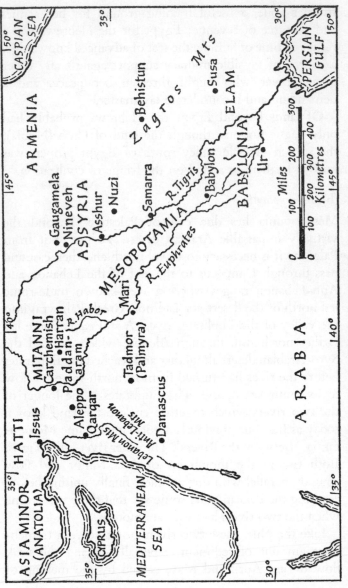

Fig. 4. Palestine and Mesopotamia

snow in the mountains. Owing to the unpredictable variations in flow, catastrophic floods, which cause great damage and may completely alter the previous course of the rivers, often ensue, particularly in the low-lying plain about 400 miles long and 125 miles broad between the head of the Persian gulf and the ancient town of Samarra, north of Baghdad. This was the area of Sumer and Akkad. Civilization first developed here under the Sumerians, a non-Semitic people of uncertain origin who occupied Sumer or Sumeria, the southern half of this area, when history began there around 4000 B.C. Then a Semitic tribe occupied Akkad, the territory north of them, and under Sargon I of Agade established the Akkadian dynasty; Akkad is the Semitic form of Agade.

North of Sumer and Akkad – which together were later called Babylonia (and in the Old Testament sometimes Shinar) – lived a mixed, though dominantly Semitic, population which eventually developed into the kingdom of Assyria. Here the two rivers flow farther apart through an area of low rainfall and, since they are well below the level of the plain, this land is at least semi-desert unless irrigated; nearer the foothills of the mountains which form the backcloth to this area rainfall increases and natural fertility made possible the support of a larger population which formed the nucleus of the state of Assyria. This kingdom took its name from the city of Asshur on the Tigris. The Assyrian and Babylonian languages are so similar that they are often called simply Akkadian; Sumerian is utterly different.

Sumer, Akkad, Babylon and Assyria and then Babylon again all in turn created empires stretching, at least in propaganda, the length of the two rivers, from the Persian gulf to the Syrian coast or, as they phrased it, 'from the Lower to the Upper Sea'. In the process they temporarily conquered or absorbed those tribes who dwelt in the highlands east of the Tigris; these were the Elamites, the Guti, the Subartu and Urartu. The Old Testament several times mentions Elam and knows also the land of Urartu in the Caucasus as the place where Noah's ark grounded (Ararat). Eventually the highlands south of the Caucasus were settled by the Indo-European Medes and Persians who then managed to conquer Mesopotamia, including the Neo-Babylonian empire whose best known ruler was Nebuchadnezzar (more correctly Nebuchadrezzar). Nebuchadnezzar exiled the inhabitants of Judah and Jerusalem; Cyrus the Persian allowed them to return.

## (c) *Hatti and Mitanni*

Non-Semitic settlers occupied the Zagros mountains and the Iranian plateau east of Mesopotamia as we have said, but at a much earlier date others had followed the mountain range westward; these were the Hittites and the Hurrians. Their importance is not evident from the Old Testament but the Hurrians (Old Testament Horites) in fact ruled the kingdom of Mitanni in the valley of the Habor and dominated Mesopotamia in the middle of the fifteenth century B.C. These Hurrians were neither Semitic nor Indo-European in language; they seem to have been widespread as peaceful settlers before a take-over by an Indo-European warrior caste turned them into a military power through the introduction of horse-chariots – for which the wide plains of northern Mesopotamia provided suitable battlefields, and the mountain lands behind them provided rearing grounds for the horses. This area seems to have been called Paddan-aram in the Old Testament, or more often Aram Naharaim, literally 'Aram of the Two Rivers' (the Euphrates and the Habor rather than the Euphrates and the Tigris).

The Hittites (or Hatti) are fairly often mentioned in the Old Testament – together with the Horites and other less easily identified peoples – as living in Palestine. But, although there do seem to have been some minor Hittite kingdoms in northern Syria, centring around Carchemish on the Euphrates, especially during the days of the monarchy in Israel, Asia Minor (sometimes called Anatolia) was their real historical home – wherever they may have come from originally – and it was there that they built up the powerful empire of Hatti during the second millennium B.C. which finally swallowed up that of Mitanni and dealt on equal terms with Egypt.

Asia Minor, for which the Old Testament has no name, is a high, square plateau rimmed especially on the north and south by still higher mountains which plunge almost directly into the sea. The lofty mountain mass of Armenia forms its eastern and only land border and on the west the mountain ranges gradually sink into the sea where the peaks of the submerged land cluster thickly off the coast to give the myriad islands of the Aegean sea. It is a land of sharp contrasts in climate as well as in physical features. Although Solomon bought horses from here (1 Kings 10: 28), on the whole there was little direct dealing between the Semites of Palestine and the Indo-European aristocracy and pre-Indo-European lower classes of Anatolia.

These were the main lands known to the Old Testament, but this list does not completely exhaust its geographical knowledge. Javan (Ionia) is mentioned, meaning the western coastlands of Asia Minor which had been settled by Greek-speaking peoples; also Caphtor (Crete) and Kittim (Cyprus) are referred to. Exotic places such as Havilah and Ophir cannot now be located; possibly very few people in ancient Palestine really knew where they were. By and large the Old Testament shows more interest in peoples than in countries. In the 'List of Nations' in Genesis 10 geographical indications are given only vaguely and racial descent is not always properly indicated; Canaanites were Semites, sons of Shem, but here they are classified as sons of Ham; the real basis of the list seems to be proximity and political connection. In a land where life was so filled with the unexpected the ancient Israelite was more concerned with his neighbours – who and where were his friends and his foes – than with matters of geography alone.

### ARCHAEOLOGICAL DISCOVERY

Archaeology is detective work in the service of history. It tries to fill up the gaps in our knowledge of past events – which is simply another way of saying 'history', because history is the story of what has happened to mankind. Sometimes the details of the story are readily available even for long ago, because they were written down and the writing, or copies of it, has been preserved to our own day. But if they were never written down or if for some other reason the tradition has been lost, we can reconstruct what happened only from clues which have been left behind, just as a detective reconstructs an event from objects found at the spot or from observable effects of the event which can be related to the incident by his trained eye and understanding mind. Such a reconstruction also helps to check the accuracy of what a witness may say happened, because a story may be unintentionally or even deliberately distorted.

Every reader of detective stories knows furthermore that there are two parts to solving a mystery and reconstructing an incident: first the evidence must be discovered and then it must be interpreted. To find something we need an eye trained to look in the right place and to recognize the sort of things we are looking for. It is also essential to note the relationship of one thing to another. This is the work of the field archaeologist – the man or woman who actually goes out and excavates a site.

When the field archaeologist has done his digging and measuring and recording he should be in a position to describe everything he has found and exactly where it was found in relation to everything else. Thereafter it does not matter if the walls he has uncovered are covered over with soil by the owner of the plot, who may want to grow vegetables there again, or that the vases and weapons and jewellery that he has so carefully dug up are taken from him to be put on display or even stacked in a cellar in a museum. As a field archaeologist his job is to gather information, not objects, and to pass this information on to the 'chair' archaeologist – often the same person is both!

The chair archaeologist takes this field information from one site and considers it in the light of relevant sections from the reports of other 'digs'. Then, with what history there is, he tries to fit it together so as to complete another small corner of the jigsaw-puzzle picture of how man used to live. Any one of us who has ever done jigsaw puzzles will know how important it is not to try to force pieces in where they do not fit, even if we have felt quite sure that that is where they should go!

5. Sites and places in Palestine

The task in archaeology is made harder because we do not have, and we never shall have, all the pieces, and because some of those we do have are damaged. Information may be incomplete because permission cannot be obtained to dig in certain places, for example under some existing buildings in Jerusalem. Earlier diggers may have messed things up so badly that no safe conclusion can be drawn. Even in a site which has been carefully excavated, past centuries of erosion by weather or more active robbing for stone or soil may have destroyed the evidence. So, in the case of the Jericho which Joshua would have seen, the mud-brick walls and houses have been washed away almost completely by the winter rains during the many years the site lay abandoned (Josh. 6: 26 and I Kings 16: 34).

## Dating

We have often been told that dates are the backbone of history, and archaeology can come to the aid of history only if it can date its discoveries, the more precisely the better. Even if written dates, as is usually the case, are not available, we can often establish a comparative date (sequence dating) because a house or temple or road which is built on top of another one must be later than the one beneath. By comparing the later with the earlier, we learn to pick out their different characteristics.

But, as in other branches of detective work, so in archaeology: there have been great advances in techniques during the present century. Probably most people have heard of the Carbon 14 method of finding out the age of any organic substance (a substance which has once been part of a living organism and so contains carbon) such as wood, bone or leather. Carefully chosen samples are subjected to an intricate analysis to find out how long

33

ago the original plant or animal material died. This test gives only approximate results and is most useful for prehistoric periods for which more exact dating evidence is not available. Another laboratory method of dating is to measure the magnetic compass declination baked into oven clay. This method relies on two observations: that magnetic north declines from true north by a fixed annual amount and that there are magnetic particles in clay which follow this declination until they are fixed by strong heat. By measuring how much magnetic north has moved, compared with the direction baked into the clay, an approximate date for the oven can be given. Because so few trees are available, dendrochronology, in which dates are reckoned by counting the annual growth rings in tree trunks, is not much used in Palestine though it may provide a check on other methods. Ceramic spectrography may be more useful, though it can only date pottery indirectly, by identifying the claypit from which the clay for a particular pot was derived. Every clay has its own chemical composition which can be identified by its spectrograph – rather like taking its fingerprint.

These newer techniques are very useful in that they give us definite dates, even if only approximate. When an object is dated by the Carbon 14 method we may be told that it is 6,000 years old ± 200, which means that it is between 6,200 and 5,800 years old. A date like this means more to the non-specialist than the other method, which classifies periods in terms not of years but of culture, such as Stone Age, Bronze Age or Iron Age and their sub-divisions. The way of classifying by culture is still very important, especially for the archaeologist, but it may confuse the non-expert because the Bronze Age in the Near East stretched roughly from 3200 to 1200 B.C., whereas in Britain it lasted from about 1900 to 500 B.C.; the aborigines in Australia were still in the Stone Age until almost within living memory because they had no metal at all. 'Ages' can only be correlated with 'years', therefore, when we know what part of the world we are dealing with; the other dating methods do not have this drawback because they give fixed dates, an absolute chronology.

### Method and site

But all these new techniques are no substitute for careful observation on the spot by the field archaeologist and without it they may even be misleading: for it is he who must note such things as later objects fallen on to an old floor which in turn covers up still earlier objects, or maybe a deep hole dug down into an earlier level and then refilled at a much later period. During a dig in Jerusalem during 1962, Iron Age material was found *underneath* very much older Bronze Age pottery, a most confusing situation later explained when it was found that the Romans had carried loads and loads of material from somewhere else in order to fill a quarry and in so doing of course reversed the chronological order of strata (see diagram on p. 36).

Where does the archaeologist look for his finds? Occasionally a lucky chance starts him off, as happened when in 1947 a wandering shepherd lad threw a stone into a cave, heard it break a pot, and so began the discovery of the Dead Sea scrolls and of the separatist community of Jews at Qumran. There was the Arab ploughman who one day in 1928 turned up a gravestone in his field at Ras Shamra on the coast of Syria. That gravestone led to our richest harvest of knowledge about the beliefs of the Canaanites, gathered from an old library in the ruins of an ancient city-kingdom called Ugarit. It is obviously impossible to look everywhere even in a small country like Palestine; the archaeologist therefore normally chooses an already identified site (Jerusalem, or Samaria, or Jericho) and tries to find out more about it, or he takes a chance on an unidentified site – and there are many such.

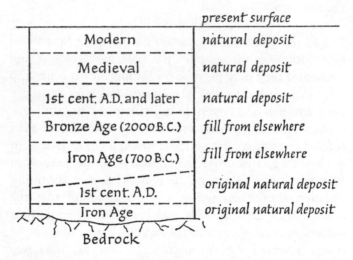

How is a site identified? Sometimes, remarkably enough, the old name still lives on even to-day in a recognizable form through all the changes of inhabitants and cultures. In Palestine this has been helped by the continuity of the basic population (wars affect the upper crust of society most) and also by the fact that the language of the country has always been some branch of Semitic speech (Canaanite, Hebrew, Aramaic or Arabic). Sometimes indeed the old name has moved to another nearby location; the present town of Jericho, for instance, (in Arabic Eriha), lies about a mile south-east of the

Old Testament site, now a deserted mound, and the ruins of Herod's Jericho are in yet another place, a mile to the south-west. Occasionally the excavator may be lucky enough to discover the name of the place he has excavated written on one of his finds. The site of Gibeon was confirmed in this way by the discovery of jar handles which had been stamped with the town's name. Where none of these aids exists, ancient writers (e.g. Eusebius, a Greek church-historian of the second century A.D., or Josephus, a Jewish historian of the first century A.D.) may have described the location of places still extant in their day, though later abandoned; or we may be able to guess at a plausible or even convincing identification from chance remarks in the Bible, as for instance that Ai was just a short distance east of Bethel (Josh. 7: 2). These latter identifications, however, are really only guesses with greater or lesser degrees of certainty. It is therefore more scientific to mention the present-day Arabic place-name alongside the conjecture; either Mizpah (Tell en-Nasbeh), or the other way round: Tell Beit Mirsim (Debir) – Tell en-Nasbeh and Tell Beit Mirsim being the present Arabic names of two ancient sites thought to be biblical Mizpah and Debir. This avoids the confusion caused by alternative identifications; for example, older books still speak of Tell el-Hesy as Lachish, whereas we now know that the true site of Lachish is almost certainly Tell ed-Duweir and that Tell el-Hesy was more probably Eglon. 'Tell' is an Arabic word for a flat-topped mound with sides which slope rather steeply. It almost always indicates the site of an ancient city and its distinctive shape is due to the practice of using the same site for city after city. To-day when new housing is built on an old site the old buildings are cleared away first; but in those days, when the higher you were the safer you felt, city re-builders just levelled off ruined buildings, threw the rubbish over the boundary wall and started building on top of the earlier town.

### Digging to-day

In the last century, excavating an ancient site might have been a hobby for the comfortably well-off amateur; nowadays, with the need for a government licence, adequate equipment and trained staff, as well as funds to pay an ever-increasing wages bill for local unskilled or semi-skilled labour, most digging is undertaken by the archaeology departments of university institutions, sometimes financially supported by public subscription and private donations.

Institutions such as local museums, which contribute to the cost of a dig, may in return receive some of the objects dug up. But the first pick, including any unique pieces, now always goes to the authorities of the country where the dig has taken place. Occasionally intrinsically valuable objects – gold, silver, jewels – are found; but mainly the objects themselves are quite unromantic – cooking-pots, mud bricks, stone walls and maybe a few coins or beads. The romance is in the story of daily occupation, trade, war or travel, which these lifeless tools will reveal to the patient student. If written material is found it is always exciting and often of great historical importance. That is why the archaeologist – even though he hands over his written finds to the *epigraphist* to be read and interpreted – always looks on both sides of every piece of pottery or flat stone he digs up and if they are dirty he has them carefully washed. Broken bits of unglazed pottery – to be had for the picking up – could be written on with pen and ink and, when the guard room at Tell ed-Duweir (Lachish) was excavated, about a score of these *ostraca* were found, containing reports to the officer-in-charge from his subordinates at other posts; they were written in Jeremiah's days at the time when Jerusalem was being threatened by the invading army of Nebuchadnezzar. A famous find at Gezer was a small, flat piece of re-used chalky stone on which some sort of calendar had been scratched, possibly as a school exercise, possibly during Solomon's reign. Many of the interesting things which have been found in Palestine by archaeologists can be seen in museums in Istanbul, Jerusalem and Amman; there is also material in London, in the British Museum and at the Institute of Archaeology, and in the U.S.A. in the Brooklyn Museum, the University of Chicago Oriental Institute, and the Museum of Fine Arts, Boston.

Many people are disappointed that, even when written material is found, it never seems to tie up directly with persons named in the Old Testament. This is not really to be wondered at. Let us for comparison take a copy of a daily newspaper and look at what it tells us; in a thousand years time how likely would it be that someone turning over the remains of a twentieth-century city would find a reference to any one of those news stories? All that could really be expected would be that what was dug up would reflect a civilization of the same sort as the one providing the news in our daily paper.

### Why have archaeology?

What does Old Testament archaeology give us? Firstly, it gives us perspective. Viewed against the many thousands of years of man's life in Palestine, the biblical period is scarcely more than an interlude, chronologically speaking. This of course does not imply that it is therefore less important. Length or quantity of time is something quite separate from the value of a period as a contribution to the enrichment of human life.

Secondly, it fills up the background of our knowledge. We can only occasionally say that archaeological discovery has proved the correctness of some historical circumstance mentioned in the Bible and of course it can never prove or disprove a *religious* truth. But very many of the discoveries enable us to understand much more fully practices, circumstances and allusions in the Bible which were so familiar to the writer and his circle that there was no need to explain them, but which have left later generations groping in the dark.

Thirdly, though this may be rather subjective, we are brought into such close physical contact – we can walk on stones showing the ruts made by Assyrian chariot wheels, we can handle a set of shopkeeper's weights or a lamp once put to lighten the gloom of a dark tomb – and these things not only bring the past alive, they also remind us that we are not so very different from our predecessors after all, and what they learnt about the science of living, which we call religion, has had a pretty thorough testing.

### Periods of culture in Palestine

We shall now briefly run through the main periods of culture and development in Palestine from as early as we can trace them, before concentrating in more detail on the comparatively fleeting centuries which are directly relevant to the archaeology of the Old Testament itself.

In 1969 the grave of a teenager was discovered in a

hillside cave near Nazareth accompanied by the bones of what was apparently a sacrificed animal. This is not in itself a very unusual find; what makes it important archaeologically is that, being dated over 50,000 years ago, it is claimed to be the oldest religious burial yet found anywhere in the world. But human beings were living in Palestine long before this and hunting elephants, rhinoceroses and hippopotamuses with flint-tipped arrows and spears. During the drier periods they lived largely on the open hillsides, but when the rainy (pluvial) periods came, which were the Ice Ages of Europe, they moved into the numerous limestone caves of the mount Carmel ridge and other similar places. In these caves the floor level gradually rose by the accumulation from year to year (even century to century!) of household rubbish: sometimes some of it was pushed out of the cave and fell in a semi-circle around its mouth. Sifting through this stuff in the early 1930s Dr Dorothy Garrod and her helpers discovered not only stone tools and animal bones – no pottery because it was not yet invented – but human skeletons which seemed to be intermediate between the Neanderthal type and a later type which is not very different from us in appearance.

After a long period of Old Stone Age hunters and food-gatherers (roughly 50,000 to 8000 B.C.) Palestine during the Middle Stone Age (Mesolithic) was inhabited by part-time farmers often called Natufians, after the wadi Natuf where some of them once lived. They were a short, slender folk who grew at least some of their own food in small patches of cleared ground and reaped their grain with flint-edged sickles. They fished and also ate meat for which they hunted; they did not have domesticated animals – except maybe the dog. Their tools and utensils show considerable development from Old Stone Age achievement; they made stone pestles and mortars and carved bone handles, beads and fasteners. Some of them continued to live in caves but others built houses with stone walls for a foundation. They may have been the first people to settle permanently on the site of Jericho.

Around 7000 B.C., after 1,000 years of gradual development, a real town with permanent houses surrounded by a strong mud-brick wall came into being at Jericho, with at least one massive stone-built tower, nearly solid but with a steep stone stair up through its centre. These people, and the succeeding group, who were highly artistic and used to model the features of their dead by overlaying their skulls with clay, had a Neolithic culture; they had no pottery but made excellent stone vessels.

Jericho, and possibly the rest of Palestine, suffered a decline in material culture from about 5000 to 3300 B.C. The people were maybe semi-nomadic and built only rather poor huts to live in although they did have pottery; their living-conditions remained unchanged to the end of the Neolithic period. When the use of metal – first copper, then bronze – spread, Palestine saw the establishment of many towns, Jericho included. Though by this time both Egypt and Mesopotamia had their own systems of writing, there is little sign of this in Palestine, except for a few examples of potters' marks on the well-made wheel-cast pottery. But Palestine must have known of its neighbours' achievement since trade was widespread between the three countries and also with Anatolia.

The vigour and technical advance of the Early Bronze Age people may be seen not only in their pottery techniques but also in their use of copper for tools and weapons. The strong fortified sites of Ai, Gezer, Jericho and Megiddo show a culture of small independent city-states rather like the picture of pre-Israelite Canaan 2,000 years later, given in the book of Judges. The numerous destructions and re-buildings of city walls in this period show that they were also a warlike, or at least a quarrelsome, people who were not above supplementing the proceeds of their own agriculture, and their barter with the donkey-trains of travelling merchants, by raids on their neighbours and the establishment of small, short-lived empires.

The settled culture of the Early Bronze Age went out about 2100 B.C. under a hail of barbarian invaders having affinities with the Beaker folk in Europe and possibly sweeping down from the north in one of those mass migrations sparked off by a food-shortage in their homeland; even Egypt fell into anarchy under their onslaught. In Palestine they have been identified with the Amorites (Num. 13:29). A strange feature is that they seem to have lavished much more care on tombs for the dead than on houses for the living, to judge by the enormous number of tombs from this Intermediate period and they almost always have a single occupant as contrasted with the family tombs of the Early Bronze Age.

About 1900 B.C. a new group of people appears, whom we may call Canaanites; since the same word also means 'merchant' they may very well have been interested in trading. Anyhow, they overran much of the country and then settled down to build and inhabit towns once more, thus ushering in the Middle Bronze Age and imposing their superior culture on the more primitive Amorites. The latter remained in the highlands while the Canaanites occupied the more fertile lowlands – if we can rely on the Hebrew tradition about them at the end of the Late Bronze Age (Num. 13: 29). What archaeological evidence there is tends to support this, even though the Amorites seem to have adopted Canaanite ways very rapidly indeed.

One reason for the rapid establishment of Middle Bronze Age culture was that the copper–tin alloy called bronze was brought into common use and replaced the much softer copper for weapons and tools. For its effect we might compare how the perfection of the process for making steel out of raw iron revolutionized industry and warfare in the last century or two of our own era.

From the biblical point of view the special interest of this Middle Bronze Age period is that it provides the background for the stories of the patriarchs Abraham, Isaac and Jacob. In the book of Genesis the patriarchs are represented as nomads and some scholars think that at least Abraham might have been an itinerant merchant (though the Bible calls him a Hebrew, not a Canaanite), travelling from centre to centre with his train of pack-asses. The sort of place he might have visited has been excavated at Tell Beit Mirsim (possibly Debir) which at that time was a well-laid-out town surrounded by a wall 10 feet thick and strengthened at intervals by strong towers. The Canaanites of this period seem to have lived in reasonable comfort, in houses consisting of several rooms, all opening off a large, roofed, living-area. Apart from their bronze tools and weapons these people – who seem to have penetrated Palestine from the north – possessed a quite new range of pottery vessels well turned on a fast wheel (now, for the first time, widely used here) and decorated with an attractive, polished red coating and even a combed pattern. But we do not know any of these people by name; they have left no inscriptions and so we are limited to a study of them as revealed by their archaeological remains. During the middle part of this Age (Middle Bronze II) Palestine appears to have been a land of reasonable prosperity, divided up into independent city-states of aggressive character, for the cities have very well-built fortifications: massive walls, a steep plastered ramp and a ditch have been found at Megiddo and Hazor.

The steep plastered ramp or *glacis* is a new feature, probably invented by, or against, a fresh wave of obviously well-armed invading peoples. Where this wave started we do not know, but again it seems to have moved south through Palestine and into Egypt and there the invaders were called Hyksos, meaning 'foreign rulers' or something similar. Judging by the evidence of personal names which have been preserved in Egyptian writings, the Hyksos were largely of Semitic stock, that is from Arabia, Palestine, Syria and northern Mesopotamia, but with a mixture of folk from further afield who were of Indo-European descent, such as Hittites and Hurrians. The Hittites had established an empire in central and eastern Anatolia (Asia Minor) about 1700 B.C.; and the Hurrians, about 1500 B.C., took possession of the wide plains around the middle reaches of the Euphrates, where they founded the kingdom of Mitanni and made much use of horse chariots for extending and defending their territory.

The break between the Middle Bronze and Late Bronze periods is one of convenience more than anything else. It is dated about 1580 B.C. because that was when

Egyptian nationalism revived sufficiently to expel the Hyksos who had been ruling there. Those expelled probably just settled in Palestine, even though they had to submit there to a certain amount of re-asserted Egyptian overlordship. During this time such towns as Tell Beit Mirsim (Debir) and Jericho were left in ruins for at least a century – nearer two in the case of Jericho – and other cities suffered also.

Although there was no basic change in culture with the coming of the Late Bronze Age, yet the prosperity of the previous age seems to have declined, probably due to Egyptian taxes, but also from the depredations of marauding bands of Habiru. Clay tablets found amongst the records of pharaoh Akhenaten and his son-in-law Tutankhamen at Tell el-Amarna record scores of complaints from local rulers in Palestine of how they are suffering from attacks by brigands who, in some cases, it is reported, are aided and abetted by certain rulers among the Canaanites themselves. Abdihiba of Jerusalem, for example, writes, 'The Habiru plunder all the king's lands'; he claims that they are even trying to capture Jerusalem and have managed to suborn Lab'ayu, prince of Shechem, from his allegiance to the pharaoh. The word 'Habiru' occurs in several forms over a wide area and a long period and the persons so described range from household servants to hired soldiers or mere tramps; they are mentioned in Near Eastern documents from the twentieth to the twelfth centuries, oftenest but not always with Semitic names. They are not, as has sometimes been said, simply the 'Hebrews' who invaded Palestine under Joshua some two centuries later, though the two words are so similar that they may have a common origin and the biblical Hebrews may have been regarded as Habiru by others. In the Old Testament the description 'Hebrew' is mainly used by non-Hebrews. This may mean that rather like the word 'gipsy' it carries a trace of patronage, or even of disapproval, perhaps because of their lack of roots.

Even though the turbulence in the political and military sphere was making eventual conquest of the land by Philistines and Israelites easier, Late Bronze Age Canaan was not without developments on the cultural side. It has already provided a lot of archaeological evidence of temples and sacred objects, such as those found at Lachish and Megiddo and Beth-shean. This was certainly a period of trade. Egyptian statues, inscriptions and scarabs are found – as well as Canaanite copies – and there is a very typical kind of bichrome (two-coloured) pottery. The light-coloured pot is ornamented with dark bands or with pictures of fish, birds or animals, each in a separate panel of the design. There are also geometrical patterns, including one often called the 'Union Jack'. But perhaps most important of all is the increasing use of writing to be noticed during this period.

The first efforts towards writing may have taken place in Palestine, as in Egypt and Mesopotamia, before 3000 B.C., if this is a correct interpretation of some very regular marks found impressed on some jar handles in Gebal (Byblos) just north of Beirut. The same site provided examples of a more developed type of writing from the first half of the second millennium in which picture signs (pictographs) have given way to conventional signs clearly influenced by contemporary Egyptian hieroglyphic style but also by Mesopotamian cuneiform practice. But it was the Late Bronze Age which saw the adoption of alphabetic writing, and the flowering of two native forms of it, somewhere in the Palestinian–Phoenician–Syrian area. First we have the alphabetic cuneiform (wedge-shaped) writing discovered in 1929 at Ras Shamra (ancient Ugarit) on the coast north of Gebal. There are hundreds of clay tablets from here and they have revolutionized our knowledge about the life of the Canaanites. So far only two inscriptions of this type have been found in Palestine itself, one on a copper knife from near mount Tabor and the other on a clay tablet found at Beth-shemesh, but they both vary sufficiently in 'hand-writing' from the normal Ugaritic tablet to suggest that they belong to a slightly different school and we may be fortunate enough to discover more in Palestine itself some day. It is quite clear that the inventor of the Ugaritic script knew about ordinary cuneiform writing as used in Mesopotamia and for the Tell el-Amarna letters; his stroke of genius was to realize that instead of the several hundred signs needed to write, syllable by syllable, in that cumbersome system he could manage with under thirty by analysing his syllables and writing each consonant separately.

Exactly the same alphabetic system was used in the other script – the one which underlies every form of alphabetic writing in general use even today. One reason for this remarkable success is that the originators of this script were not hampered by the tradition that writing had to be done by pressing a triangular depression into a soft clay tablet with a stick; and so their pictographs, being originally done in fine ink lines with a pen on a smooth hard surface, developed into a neat, easily-remembered alphabet. The date for the invention of this linear alphabet, often linked with Phoenicia, has been gradually pushed back, perhaps into the Middle Bronze period (i.e. before 1500 B.C.), but written material from Palestine itself never becomes very plentiful even by the end of the Late Bronze period. However, we have a couple of short inscriptions from Lachish and one or two others before we come down into the Iron Age.

About 1200 B.C. once again there burst on the civilized world an advancing wave of new tribes, and the Late Bronze Age in Palestine went out under the attacks of the 'Sea Peoples', of whom the Philistines are the best known and of most concern to us. They arrived from the islands and coastal areas of the north-eastern Mediterranean and settled in Canaan, which was later on known as Palestine which is a is a modified form of Philistia. Their first objective had been Egypt, but pharaoh Rameses III managed to defeat them in a great sea-battle in 1196 B.C. off the mouth of the Nile, and diverted them to the coastland of Palestine where they settled down in five main centres, Ashdod, Ashkelon, Ekron, Gath and Gaza (I Sam. 6: 17).

It appears, though, from the Tell el-Amarna letters that there were some Philistines – or at least Sherdens, another of the Sea Peoples – already in Palestine before 1196 B.C., having been hired by the Egyptians to man their frontier posts. If so, this would explain the pre-twelfth-century presence of typically Philistine remains at Sharuhen (Tell Fara), decorated pottery and distinctive tombs which, along with Late Bronze Age objects, contained a dagger and a knife with blades of iron. At Beth-shean, too, an Egyptian frontier post, as well as at Sharuhen, coffins were found made from baked clay and having lids with human features and arms moulded into the clay. This is a type known to have been used in

Egypt by groups of Sherden soldiery over quite a long period. Some clay tablets from the mid-twelfth century, and inscribed with an unusual form of writing, were discovered in 1964 at a site called Deir Alla in the mid-Jordan valley, and some believe that these also may be directly or indirectly connected with the Philistines.

But however widespread these outposts of Sea Peoples may have been even in the Late Bronze Age and however far their typical wares may have spread by trade, when they settled as refugees *en masse* in Palestine their main area of occupation was along the Mediterranean seaboard. This is shown most clearly by the spread of their distinctive pottery. Their northern boundary was probably the Carmel ridge, because not a great deal of this pottery has come to light in Megiddo. The Egyptian tale of Wen Amun, however, indicates that a branch of the Sea Peoples called Tjekker held the area south of mount Carmel with its port of Dor, and their contemptuous treatment of Wen Amun, an Egyptian envoy, shows how low Egyptian prestige had fallen.

The eastern boundary of the Philistines fluctuated with the victories and defeats which punctuated their struggles with the other invaders who were trying to occupy Palestine at the same time, but from the landward side. These were the Israelites. Most disappointingly for us there is little of this struggle which can be traced archaeologically, since the cities which can be shown to have been destroyed at this period – such as Ashkelon – were of course inhabited by Canaanites and it is very difficult to tell a Philistine destruction from an Israelite or any other one.

## Israelites in Palestine

Fortunately, though quite by chance, we are able to prove the presence of Israelites in Palestine from the famous stele of Merenptah, a monument upon which that pharaoh inscribed a poem to celebrate his victories in war. Near the end he boasts that 'The people Israel is devastated, his offspring exist not'. This is the only mention of Israel ever found on an Egyptian monument, yet it does show that Israel was important enough to be mentioned in despatches from Palestine, even though at that time (about 1230 B.C.) the Israelites were probably still at least semi-nomadic.

This proof of their presence is the more important since otherwise 'with one exception there is no evidence, in the proper sense of the word, that a new ethnic group was taking over power in the land at this time'. The archaeologist H. J. Franken is speaking here of the results of archaeological digging and his 'one exception' refers to a chain of small settlements in upper Galilee which were founded during the early Iron Age at an apparently intentional distance from the Canaanite Late Bronze Age cities of the area. The deduction is that these small settlements were peopled by an incoming wave too weak in numbers or equipment to compete with the existing holders of the land. This reminds us of the statement that the northern tribes of Israel were unable to dislodge the Canaanites from their fortified cities and had to take up residence where they could (Judg. 1: 27–35).

Lack of clear information from archaeological investigation is not final, nor does it leave us at a complete loss. We can still look forward to finding much more and clearer evidence in the ground when others of the scores of still undug sites are scientifically examined. Furthermore, with the coming of the Israelites into Palestine, we move into a period where written records begin to help and archaeology as such becomes more of a check upon, and a supplement to, written history than a substitute for it.

In the biblical account of the exodus from Egypt and the wandering in the wilderness, the whole twelve tribes of Israel seem to have taken forty years after leaving Egypt to arrive at or near the mouth of the river Jordan; but archaeology has so far come up with very meagre information about this period and that mostly negative. In a series of surface surveys between 1933 and 1946 Nelson Glueck examined a number of sites in Transjordan and from the pottery he found scattered on the surface he concluded that Edom and Moab had no settled population between about 2000 and 1300 B.C. Doubts are now cast on this evidence, but if he was right and if the tradition is sound that the Israelites were opposed by an army of settled Edomites on their way to invade Canaan (Num. 20: 20–1), then the exodus could not have been earlier than 1300 B.C. But, once across Jordan, the biblical narrative mentions definite sites in Palestine and some of these have been archaeologically investigated, sometimes with puzzling results.

The first of these sites is Jericho, in whose case the evidence from the series of excavations by Dr Kathleen Kenyon from 1952 to 1958 must be used to correct the imperfect results of previous expeditions. This town, whose history goes back further than any other yet excavated, was destroyed and abandoned about 1580 B.C. and Dr Kenyon tells us that, although some occupation may have begun again about 1400 B.C., that city too was later destroyed and almost no trace of it can now be found, because winter rains have washed away its mud-brick walls and summer winds have blown away the crumbled clay. We shall never be able to reconstruct from the actual ruins a model of the town which Joshua's spies would have seen, nor measure its fallen walls. Neither can we get much help toward dating the Israelite attack; 1400 B.C. seems to be too early on any current theory of the date of the exodus and, if there has been a later city on the site, all trace of it has vanished. The tradition that Joshua laid a curse on the place (Josh. 6: 26) may offer a reason for its abandonment.

After Jericho the Israelites, according to the biblical account, eventually captured Ai – a peculiar name for a city, since it means 'ruin'! Owing to the description of its position (Josh. 7: 2) it is usually identified with a site now called et-Tell, 'the mound', but recent excavations have confirmed earlier reports that Ai had been a ruin since the Early Bronze Age (about 2500 B.C.) until it was re-occupied in the Iron Age as an open village, around 1200 B.C. The impossibility of squaring this evidence with the account of Ai as a Late Bronze Age city has led some scholars to suppose that what was originally the capture of Bethel has been transferred by tradition to this nearby, much more impressive, mound. The main argument in favour is that Bethel (modern Beitin) was destroyed by fire, probably during the thirteenth century: in the biblical account this was done by Israelites, yet Joshua's army unaccountably seems to ignore its existence; on the other hand the story in Judges 1: 22–6 which tells us that Bethel was destroyed by the tribes of Joseph never mentions Ai.

Other cities in central Palestine, mentioned in the biblical account of the conquest, which have been examined, have not supplied evidence to confirm or disprove the biblical account; but it is interesting to note that at Shechem (Josh. 8: 30–5; 24) the transition from Late Bronze to Iron Age seems to have been peaceful and there is no mention of military conquest here at this period in the biblical narrative, except for the Abimelech incident (Judg. 9: 1–49) for which evidence has not been found.

A site which has often been quoted as showing Philistine destruction of an Israelite occupation is Shiloh (Seilun), the religious centre of Israel immediately before the monarchy and maybe adopted as such considerably earlier (Josh. 18: 1; Judg. 21: 19). Excavations carried out around 1930 seemed to show that this site had been destroyed about 1050 B.C. and it was supposed that the Philistines had followed up their defeat of Israel's army in the field (1 Sam. 4: 10–11) by capturing and sacking Shiloh; but now it appears, from further excavations in 1963 and more careful interpretation, that the terrible destruction of Shiloh mentioned by the prophet Jeremiah (7: 12; 26: 6) took place in the sixth century, probably at the hands of the Babylonians.

In southern Palestine the two most fully excavated sites mentioned in the conquest narrative are Debir, also named Kiriath-sepher (Josh. 15: 15–17; Judg. 1: 11–13), and Lachish (Josh. 10: 31–2). Although there is no absolute proof, the identification of Debir with Tell Beit Mirsim is generally accepted and the destruction of the Late Bronze Age city – dated by the pottery to about 1225 B.C. – is attributed to the Israelites because cult images had been defaced, obviously on purpose.

Lachish (Josh. 10: 31–2) has provided very useful information for Israelite history towards the end of the monarchy, but it also shows a destruction level which may be dated by an inscribed bowl to 1220 B.C. or a little later, which would therefore bring it into the same period as the destruction of Tell Beit Mirsim, though the former does not seem to have been re-occupied for over a century and opinion is unsettled as to whether it was the Israelites or the Philistines who burnt the city.

In north Palestine we have already mentioned the occupation of a number of small, somewhat unimportant, sites by an incoming Iron Age population and this fits in with what we are told in the Bible, that the Israelites were unable to reduce the fortified Canaanite cities (Josh. 11: 13). The one exception was the very important centre Hazor (Josh. 11: 10–11). Recent excavations there have proved most instructive. A city had existed on this site since Early Bronze Age days and grew to its greatest extent at the beginning of the Late Bronze Age. After that date (about 1500 B.C.) Hazor seems to have decreased in size until it was destroyed and burnt, according to the excavator, by Joshua about 1230 B.C. The period of the Israelite judges shows only meagre remains, but in the tenth century king Solomon built a massive defensive wall around one half of the previous upper-city level. The whole of this area was then walled in, once more, in the days of Ahab (ninth century); at the same time a huge tunnel was driven down through the mound itself and the underlying rock until it tapped the water table at a depth of some 42 metres. This tremendous feat of engineering – the tunnel is more than twice as big as the water tunnel at Megiddo, which was planned to reach a known spring – shows that by the ninth century the once nomadic Israelites had developed into skilled hydraulic engineers.

Little more needs to be said about the archaeology of the years when Israel was settling in Palestine, though it might be useful to remind ourselves of the background of the Song of Deborah (Judg. 5 and compare also Judg. 4). Whatever the immediate cause of the uprising called by Deborah and led by Barak, its purpose seems to have been the unification of the centre of Palestine with the north by destroying, or at least weakening, the row of fortified cities – Dor, Megiddo, Taanach, Ibleam and Beth-shean – which kept them apart. Reuben, Gilead (Gad), Dan and Asher are chided for not sending a contingent to the battle (presumably because they felt it was too far off to be their concern); but the southern tribes, Judah, Simeon and Levi, are not blamed even though Judah was no further away than Reuben was. The reason is that another west-to-east chain of non-Israelite cities cut them off, including Gezer, Aijalon and Jerusalem.

*Capital cities of the Israelite kings*

Since from this time Israelite history can be more fully reconstructed from the written records than from the finds of archaeology, we shall now merely point out a few instances where archaeology serves to illustrate, correct or supplement the written record. We might first run through the capitals of the various kings of Israel. Omitting for the moment Shechem, which was the capital of the half-Canaanite king Abimelech (Judg. 9), we find that Saul had his centre at Gibeah, usually identified with the hill-top village called Tell el-Fûl, only 3 miles north of Jerusalem, which in Saul's day was still in Canaanite hands. The earliest village on this site dates from the Iron Age (early twelfth century) so it was probably Israelite from the start; it had a rough, strongly-built tower or small castle at its centre whose upper part was of wood (cypress and pine). This was earlier than the time of Saul and it must have been destroyed by foreign marauders or in a battle during some family feud, such as the one recorded in Judges 20: 36–40. Whether Saul or his father rebuilt its stronghold we do not know, but it too was a very unpretentious royal palace and reflects the poverty of material culture among the early Israelites.

The three cities which served as the capital of the northern kingdom after the disruption were Shechem (1 Kings 12: 25), Tirzah (1 Kings 14: 17; 15: 21) and Samaria (1 Kings 16: 24) and all three have been excavated. Shechem has already figured as an important city in early Israelite history (Gen. 12: 6f.; Josh. 24; Judg. 9) as well as in the Tell el-Amarna letters. There is no doubt that it was the most important city of the northern kingdom, situated as it was at the eastern opening of the east-to-west pass between mount Ebal to the north and mount Gerizim to the south, and adjoining the central north-to-south route as well. It also had a very famous pre-Israelite shrine to the God of Covenant, Baal- or El-berith (Judg. 9: 4, 46). Excavation has shown that the city was very strongly fortified during the Middle and Late Bronze Ages and that it had a sacred area on which several consecutive temples were later built; these temples were strongly fortified buildings which would serve like a castle keep for a last stand (Judg. 9: 46). An interesting find in the last Bronze Age temple on the site was a large white stone trimmed to roughly 18 inches thick and 54 inches wide; its original height is unknown as it had been broken off about 54 inches from the bottom when found. It was undoubtedly a *massebah* (Gen. 28: 18), a symbol most often regarded as sacred to Baal and thus frowned upon by orthodox Yahweh worshippers (Exod. 34: 13), but it could well be that the tradition linking the name of Joshua with a great stone set up in the Shechem sanctuary has this very stone in mind. The excavator of the site has pointed out that not only is there no record of the invading Israelites destroying Shechem or even conquering it, but the excavation showed no break in occupation after about 1450 B.C. (too early for Joshua) until about 1100 B.C. (too late for Joshua and better suited to the destruction wrought by Abimelech – Judg. 9: 45).

The archaeological evidence that Shechem was rebuilt during Solomon's days is borne out by the statement that 'Rehoboam went to Shechem, for all Israel had gone there to make him king' (1 Kings 12: 1) and the continuing importance of this city is shown by its being chosen by Jeroboam for his first capital (verse 25). The new glory was shortlived for, although the Bible does not say so, Shechem was destroyed again seven times between Jeroboam's successful revolt and the first quarter of the fifth century B.C. It may have been pharaoh Shishak's raid through Palestine in 924 B.C. (1 Kings 14: 25) which destroyed Shechem so soon; the unearthed fragment of the inscription Shishak set up at Megiddo does not actually mention it but it does include Penuel, the place to which Jeroboam went from Shechem (1 Kings 12: 25). It could well have been the destruction of Shechem, his new capital, that made Jeroboam fear that his people would revert to Jerusalem (1 Kings 12: 26) and it is striking that he apparently had to abandon any hope of keeping to the sacred tradition of the Shechemite sanctuary and chose instead Dan and Bethel, at the northern and southern borders respectively of his kingdom (verse 29).

Although Shechem lost much of its pre-eminence in the centuries after Jeroboam and was apparently abandoned by its inhabitants about 475 B.C., the invasion of Alexander the Great seems to have led to its being rebuilt and fortified on a large scale. The reason advanced for this is that Alexander destroyed Samaria in 331 B.C. and, since that site was then given to some of his Macedonian troops, the displaced Samaritans seem to have moved to the old site of Shechem and there they remained until they moved from the old site on the valley floor and, on the flank of mount Gerizim, built a 'new city' (Greek *Neapolis* which has become, in Arabic, Nablus), where the remnant of them still lives. When the temple on mount Gerizim was built – or exactly where – we do not know. Excavations have revealed remains going back to the hellenistic period on a knoll of the mountain overlooking the town, but the earlier main Canaanite sanctuary was in Shechem itself.

We do not know how long Jeroboam stayed in Penuel; the next home town attributed to him is Tirzah (1 Kings 14: 17), a site only 7 miles north-east of Shechem if, as seems very probable, we may identify it with Tell el-Farah. The fertility of this area led to its development as an encampment, rather than anything worthy to be called a town, as early as the Neolithic period, though occupation became more marked in the following Chalcolithic age in which bronze was used as well as stone. The dwellings of these people were mere pits sunk into the ground, presumably with some sort of flimsy tent or brushwood cover, and we know nothing of their furniture, but they have left one of the most representative collections of Upper Chalcolithic pottery yet found. But circumstances changed; in the Early Bronze Age a fortified town with straight streets and mud-brick houses on stone foundations testifies to a much higher stage in civilization beginning here about 3100 B.C., probably as a result of invasion. A very interesting find, dating from the middle of this period, was a potter's kiln. This has a strong claim to being one of the oldest in Palestine.

Occupation of Tell el-Farah temporarily ceased about 2600 B.C. We do not know whether this was caused by invading Amorites or was perhaps due to the prevalence of malaria there. Unfortunately the Middle and Late Bronze Age buildings on this site are not well preserved, but there is a gateway through the city wall – though this may belong to the Iron Age – which seems to have had a bench in it so that people could sit in the shade of the tunnel-like entrance (Ruth 4: 1). A sad discovery was the skeleton of a baby placed in a jar and buried in the foundations of the entrance, as too in Shechem at the same period. Perhaps it was a foundation sacrifice; 1 Kings 16: 34 may refer to this practice, which is known elsewhere in the ancient world.

The Israelites were forbidden in their Law (Lev. 11: 7; Isa. 65: 4) to eat pig meat and it has often been suggested that the reason may have been that it was a favourite sacrifice to Canaanite gods. The excavator of Tell el-Farah unearthed very many bones of young pigs in an underground room interpreted as a sanctuary dedicated to an agricultural god or goddess; its date would be between 1800 and 1500 B.C.

Too little remains to show how or when the Israelites

took over this site, but they seem to have been in possession by the time of David and to have established a long-continuing and clearly-laid-out town with street after street of rather stereotyped houses each occupying a plot roughly 30 feet square; a door from the street led into a courtyard with rooms on each side opening off it – a typical Mediterranean family house-plan.

Jeroboam's successors continued to reign from Tirzah, but it was a time of revolution and counter-revolution and the city was almost destroyed, apparently before Omri decided to move his capital to Samaria (1 Kings 16: 24). After a short period Tirzah rose again and reflected in its buildings not only the increasing wealth of the eighth century but also the growing gulf between rich and poor (Amos 5: 11–12; 8: 4–6). This city was destroyed at the time of the Assyrian invasion which ended the northern kingdom. The conquerors settled an Assyrian colony here later, but it never seems to have flourished, it was not allowed to have any fortifications to protect it and it finally petered out about the time that Judah too lost her own independent existence.

The one great difference between Samaria (modern Sebastiye) and the other cities mentioned is that here we have for the first time a city whose first founder was an Israelite. According to 1 Kings 16: 24 Omri bought the site from its owner and proceeded to build a new capital for himself which he named Samaria. The earliest record of this name is an Assyrian inscription of Adad-Nirari III which records that he exacted tribute from 'Joash of Samaria' in 798 B.C., roughly eighty years later. The Bible derives the name Samaria from that of the previous owner of the site, Shemer: but in view of the hill's impressive elevation above its surrounding fertile meadows, it would have been natural to connect it with the verb *shamar* (to watch, to guard). The reasons for choosing this site – apart from its much healthier position – would seem to have been its much better communications with the western half of the kingdom and its better protection from the east and possible Aramaean pressure.

The ruins of the palace built by Omri, or his son Ahab, have been discovered. It formed part of a royal quarter facing west on the upper part of the hill and though it was not particularly large nor very different in plan from the typical Israelite house with a central courtyard, the workmanship of the limestone masonry is extraordinarily good and the rising wealth of the kingdom is shown by the finding on the site of numerous fragments of ivory inlay. These illustrate the biblical references to 'houses of ivory' and 'beds inlaid with ivory' (1 Kings 22: 39; Amos 3: 15; 6: 4).

Maybe it was in the square tower which once guarded the approach to the western gate that Pekahiah was assassinated by Pekah (2 Kings 15: 25). The round towers here and on the eastern approach are much later. Another discovery of a feature mentioned in the Bible was the pool (1 Kings 22: 38) in the northern part of the royal quarter; but the town itself has not yet been excavated. Another rare find was that made in 1910 of sixty-three invoices for wine and oil written on bits of unglazed pot from the reign of Jeroboam II. This discovery was supplemented in 1932 by a few more, probably slightly later in date, one of which recorded the sale of some barley. It is a pity that the contents do not tell us more about Samaria in general, but they show that business affairs – perhaps taxgathering in kind – were conducted in a well-organized and documented way, which reminds us that one of the earliest if not *the* earliest use for writing was for listing contributions to the upkeep of government and religion.

Samaria was the last, as well as the most important, capital of the northern kingdom. Sargon II, king of Assyria, claimed to have captured Samaria in 722 or 721 B.C. immediately after the death of his predecessor Shalmaneser V who had begun the three-year siege of the city in 725 B.C. (2 Kings 17: 1–6; 18: 9–10). In fact Sargon may not have been actually king when Samaria fell, but little trace of any destruction remains at this time, or of the restorations and improvements he claims to have made. One reason for this is that in 107 B.C. John Hyrcanus destroyed the walls of the hellenistic city of his day and there was extensive erosion of the whole site during the following years. The Roman proconsul Gabinius helped to rebuild the city, but when it was presented by Augustus to Herod in 30 B.C. Herod 'developed' it in quite the modern sense as a Greek city, renaming it Sebaste in honour of his patron Augustus, whose name would be Sebastos if translated into Greek.

There is a great deal more still to be learnt from future excavations, not only about Omri's settlement near the crest of the hill but also about how the city grew, and what lay within the line of its yellow limestone walls. Maybe we shall find some tangible remains, too, belonging to the Samaria of the Sanballat who created difficulties for Nehemiah (Neh. 2: 10), and perhaps some more documents like the forty or so papyri discovered in a cave north of Jericho which seem to have been brought there from Samaria by people who were trying to escape the soldiers of Alexander. Among the information these business documents provide is the fact that there were at least three different governors of Samaria called Sanballat. Yet already we know at least as much about the archaeology of Samaria as of the other capitals of the northern kingdom.

When we turn to the southern kingdom three cities deserve to rank as the capital at some period, if we ignore the short tenure of office at Mizpah exercised by Gedaliah, the governor of Judah appointed by the Babylonians (Jer. 40: 5–6). Gibeah (Tell el-Fûl) the centre of Saul's rule has already been described. After Saul's death David took up residence at Hebron where he was anointed king, first over Judah only (2 Sam. 2: 4), and then over Israel also (2 Sam. 5: 3). So far we have little archaeological evidence available about these and later Israelite events at Hebron and so we must turn our attention to Jerusalem. Details about Jerusalem have been more sought after than those of any other city, from the days of queen Helena, the first Christian Roman empress, down to the present day.

Pictures of Jerusalem usually show a very picturesque and antique-looking walled city. Indeed it used to be possible to walk round 'the old city' as it is called, without descending from these walls. But these walls were built by the Turkish ruler Suleiman the Magnificent in A.D. 1538–41. It is true that he built very largely on the foundations of the city's wall from a much earlier period, and excavations at his Damascus gate, which is the main entrance from the north, have shown that he built there on stones laid by the Roman emperor Hadrian when he turned Jerusalem into a Roman city in A.D. 135. Underneath the work of Hadrian, in turn, was a gateway built by Herod Agrippa about A.D. 42 which takes us back

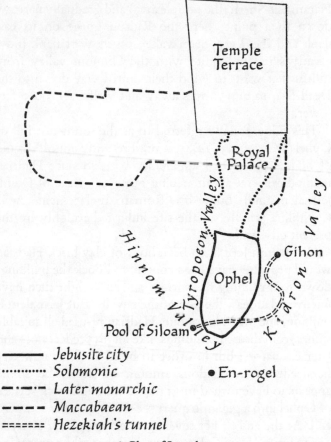

6. Plan of Jerusalem

to New Testament times before the siege and destruction
of Jewish Jerusalem in A.D. 70 by Titus.

But much of New Testament Jerusalem and probably
most of the Old Testament city lay south of the present
walled part and we must look for it on the flat top of the
curving ridge which starts against the south wall of the

Haram esh-Sherif (the temple area) and gradually narrows down to a point; here the Kidron gorge on its east flank and the Tyropoeon valley on its west flank (now greatly silted up) unite with the Hinnom valley from still further west, to wind their united way down to the Dead Sea, 12 or 15 miles away and well over 3,000 feet lower.

This ridge, usually referred to as the south-east hill or Ophel (2 Chron. 33 : 14), was until recently almost devoid of buildings and had apparently been so since Hadrian methodically set about wiping out every trace of Jewish Jerusalem and built his Roman replacement Aelia Capitolina wholly on the site indicated roughly by the present city wall.

Had Jewish Jerusalem been built of clay brick Hadrian would probably have been content to knock the buildings down to a roughly flat surface and we might then have uncovered at least the line of their walls. But Jerusalem is built on, and with, limestone. Hadrian re-used all suitable stones from disused buildings, like all his predecessors and later emulators; but in order to build a whole new city he needed a tremendous amount of stone and so he appears to have turned most of the accessible rock surface of Ophel into a gigantic quarry, especially at the southern end. At the end of her seven-year campaign Dr Kenyon had to write, 'David's Jerusalem, and that of the preceding Jebusites, has thus virtually vanished.'

However, excavation has not drawn a complete blank by any means. Basing ourselves mainly on the results of Dr Kenyon's investigations, which supplement and often correct earlier work, we find that when king David captured Jerusalem (2 Sam. 5: 6–10; 1 Chron. 11: 4–9) the Jebusites who lived there had built a wall as low down as they could on the eastern side of Ophel. They could not safely build it low enough down to enclose the only spring thereabouts, but they channelled the water back from the spring through a tunnel which they cut into the hill until they could sink a shaft inside the wall to meet the tunnel and draw water that way, safe from the sling-stones and arrows of their enemies. This water shaft has been known for a hundred years, but the Jebusite town wall between it and the Gihon spring was only uncovered in 1962. David seems to have taken it over and it seems to have served well for his successors also as the replacement for it, standing a few feet higher up the slope, appears to date from a time soon after the days of the prophet Isaiah. Owing to imperfect dating methods, many of the walls found by earlier excavators were attributed to the days of David or Solomon when, in reality, they were much later, sometimes even Maccabaean, including the massive tower on the very edge of the plateau directly above the spring Gihon.

Solomon is famous for his building projects in Jerusalem (1 Kings 6 and 7). His palace backed on to the temple and it may be that the present Dome of the Rock (sometimes still called the Mosque of Omar) stands at the same spot. Solomon's temple was destroyed by Nebuchadnezzar (2 Kings 25: 8–9) in 586 B.C. and then replaced by a less impressive one (Hag. 2: 3) after the exile. This served until Herod decided to build a new one which would raise his own prestige. To give it an impressive setting he greatly extended the temple court southward. To do this he had to raise the level of the ground and he must have permanently covered up any traces of Solomon's palace which might still have existed; though a massive north-to-south wall discovered not far from the temple enclosure might conceivably have marked the eastern boundary of Solomon's royal quarter.

Other old walls have been discovered during different excavations of Jerusalem, but their dates and exact purposes are often difficult to ascertain owing to the constant building and rebuilding which went on. However, one of the several city walls on the eastern slope of Ophel must have been built, or at least repaired, by Hezekiah to withstand the army sent by Sennacherib, king of Assyria (2 Kings 18: 13 ff.; Isa. 36). It was probably at this time too that the Siloam tunnel was dug, on a rather winding course, right through the Ophel hill, to take the water from the Gihon spring already mentioned into a reservoir on the west side of Ophel called the Pool of Siloam (2 Kings 20: 20). This pool may, at that time, have been in a sort of underground cave and so well protected from attack. Nowadays, except after heavy rain, it is possible to walk down a flight of stone steps at the Gihon end and wade some 500 metres through the tunnel, eventually emerging into the present-day shallow, open-air pool from which the water flows to irrigate the fertile gardens and orchards lower down the valley.

Hezekiah also 'suppressed the hill-shrines, smashed the sacred pillars' (2 Kings 18: 4). The hill-shrines were usually those of heathen gods or goddesses and the sacred pillars were standing stones which represented Baal the god of nature and stood near the altar in the shrine. How many of these shrines Hezekiah destroyed we are not told, but one which he could have known was recently unearthed just outside the eastern wall of Ophel. It had two of these standing stones in a small room, with what could have been an altar on a wide shelf of rock on a higher level; near at hand, in a cave which had been walled up and re-opened several times, was found a collection of very well-preserved jugs and bowls which perhaps had once been used in the shrine. Unfortunately no details about the actual worshippers have been preserved; these cults seem to have had quite a hold on the people throughout the monarchy and the large number of small clay models, both human and animal, which are found in excavations throughout Palestine, as well as in Jerusalem, probably played a part in the more popular forms of worship as charms or for magic spells.

Nebuchadnezzar in 586 B.C. burnt the main buildings of Jerusalem to the ground and broke down its defensive walls. When Nehemiah obtained permission in 445 B.C. to rebuild the walls he found that the going on the east slope of Ophel was so rugged that he could not proceed. The destruction of the city wall near the foot of the slope had meant that the terraces of houses built inside and above it on the steep hillside had simply tumbled down in a heap, where many of them still lie. Since Nehemiah had to house a much smaller population than the pre-exilic one he decided to cut his losses, and for the eastern boundary of the city he built his wall along the top edge of the slope, where some of its foundations have been uncovered beneath a later, Maccabaean, wall. It was possible to date the lower part of the wall to the fifth century B.C. by means of the rubbish which lay against its outer side.

Nehemiah's Jerusalem therefore seems to have been the smallest on record, consisting as it did of the comparatively flat summit of Ophel; but to the north of it there was also, of course, the temple, rebuilt in the days of Haggai and Zechariah. Some of the masonry in the retaining wall on the eastern side of this temple area may perhaps be of the Persian period and, if this is so, then it may be that after all we do have some remains of the second temple still visible – and this may allow the hope that still more of the ancient city of Jerusalem will yet come to light.

## THE HISTORICAL PERSPECTIVE

Anyone setting out to write about the past chooses what seems to him important for his purpose and leaves out what might well be important for another author writing with another interest. Every history book tells only part of a much more complex and varied story. The Old Testament has been written mainly to tell about the religious history of Israel, but a considerable amount of political and economic history is included.

The Israelites regarded some of the events of the past as very important because of the lessons which had been drawn from them and a good deal of factual material was available when the historical parts of the Old Testament were written. This is shown by the number of different sources that are named, such as the Book of the Wars of the LORD (Num. 21: 14), the annals of Solomon (1 Kings 11: 41) and those of the kings of Israel (1 Kings 14: 19) and of Judah (1 Kings 14: 29), even the history of Nathan the prophet (2 Chron. 9: 29). None of these sources is available for us to consult; we should have a good deal more detailed information if they were and it is worth thinking about what difference this might make to us, particularly if we had these *instead* of the Old Testament. Clearly the writers depended on other

sources also which are not named but which stand out
from their context because of the way in which they
were used. For instead of rewriting everything the common practice was to take a whole section out of the
earlier work and re-use it with only so much added as
was needed to make it suit its new position. In the book
of Judges, for example, it is quite easy to see the difference
between the editor's introduction 'Once more the
Israelites did what was wrong in the eyes of the LORD,
and he delivered them into the hands of the Philistines
for forty years' (Judg. 13: 1) and the story he then
proceeds to tell. The story (Judg. 13: 2 – 16: 31) then ends
with another very short editorial statement, 'He had
been judge over Israel for twenty years.'

Sometimes two slightly different accounts of the same
incident have been combined but the differences remain
clearly visible. This suggests that there was no means of
deciding between them and perhaps also that this kind
of detail did not seem to be very important. One obvious
example of this is in the story of Joseph where sometimes
Reuben, sometimes Judah, takes Joseph's side (Gen.
37: 21–30). The two very different accounts of how and
why Saul became king of Israel remain separate but
close to one another in 1 Samuel (9: 1 – 10: 16 and 8; 10:
17–27).

Besides the royal annals and prophetic records there
was probably a great deal of material still not written
down but preserved in oral tradition. Most peoples have
had a period when stories of the past were handed on by
word of mouth and long and complicated narratives
have been memorized and handed down from generation
to generation before being written down. Maybe this
was what happened to the stories about the patriarchs

and the judges and, even after they were written down, the stories would still be remembered and recited, as indeed they still are.

The books of Joshua, Judges, Samuel and Kings are reckoned among the prophetical books in the Jewish tradition. The prophets certainly had a good deal to say about history as it was being made in their own times as well as about the traditions that had been handed down from the past and these books were compiled by writers deeply under the influence of the prophets. From a modern point of view their books can scarcely be called 'historical' and it would perhaps be better if this description could be discarded. On the other hand the label does secure the point that they are concerned with actual happenings and the way in which what men do affects the welfare and the future of society.

The knowledge we now have of the history of the ancient Near East makes it possible to put the stories against a background, if we can find a suitable one. The stories of the patriarchs reflect a background which we may call historical because it corresponds with what we know about the period of Aramaean migration between Mesopotamia and Palestine during the Middle Bronze Age, that is, about 1850 B.C. Some of the practices mentioned in the stories were known at Nuzi in northern Mesopotamia at this period. In the stories in Genesis there are no precise links with any particular date or place and we cannot go on from saying that these things *could* have happened at this time to saying that they actually *did* happen as they are narrated. (See *Old Testament Illustrations*, pp. 34 f.)

## The exodus from Egypt

When we come to the book of Exodus we come nearer to history, even though many scholars feel that myth, dramatization and exaggeration have so heightened the effect that historical elements are difficult to identify. But to suppose that the sojourn in Egypt, the leadership of Moses and the exodus itself were invented by later Israelites creates more problems than it solves. There can be little doubt that ancestors of Israel were held as slaves in Egypt and did escape in a way which to them was so marvellous that they saw in it the hand of God working on their behalf.

But the actual course of events is still unclear. There is still disagreement about when the Israelites' ancestors reached Egypt, how many of the tribes were ever in Egypt, even about when they made their escape. The reasons for the uncertainty are two: in the first place there is no direct non-biblical evidence for Moses or for the escape; secondly, even if the biblical writers knew of traditions which would shed light on these points, they were not primarily interested in facts such as these, and so preserved almost exclusively those details which lighted up what they believed to be the inner meaning of the events. There are indications that the exodus story was told or acted in later years by the Israelites as a kind of miracle play to remind them of how God had looked after them in the past. For the Israelites this had been their beginning as a nation and as worshippers of Yahweh; its importance was emphasized and re-emphasized in the telling and retelling. But for the Egyptians a quite insignificant revolt and the escape of some Hebrew slaves would soon be forgotten and never recorded.

73

Three pieces of evidence support the view that the ancestors of the Israelites spent some time in Egypt. A number of early Israelites had Egyptian names, Hophni, Phinehas, Merari and particularly Moses himself and maybe Aaron. The word corresponding to 'Hebrew', 'Apiru' or 'Khapiru', is found in Egyptian texts and is used for a conscript force engaged in public works during the New Kingdom (fifteenth to twelfth centuries B.C.): there is nothing to prove or disprove the identity of the biblical Hebrews with the Apiru and in any case the same term – in the form 'Habiru' – is found all over the Near East at this period and is used of people who cannot possibly be the biblical Hebrews. The third piece of evidence relates to the statement 'This is how Pharaoh's store-cities, Pithom and Rameses, were built' (Exod. I: II). A store-city Rameses was known by that name between 1290 and 1100 B.C. and if the slaves were at work there the tradition could have taken form between these dates. But Rameses built a number of cities which he named after himself, so this cannot be very conclusive.

Of the dates proposed for the exodus itself, one in the thirteenth century (1290 or 1230 B.C.) is most widely accepted today because, although it cannot be said to agree with all of it, it agrees with more of the evidence than the other dates (e.g. 1580 or 1450 B.C.). The genealogy of Moses in Numbers 26: 59 makes him the grandson of Joseph's brother Levi, which would make it possible that the Israelites came into Egypt during the reign of the pharaoh Akhenaten some time after 1400 B.C. when they might well have been favourably received. This means that we must ignore the figure of 430 years in Exodus 12: 40, but no simple conclusion can be reached in which all the alternatives are reconciled.

Though one group of tribes went to Egypt and was led out again perhaps a century and a half later by Moses, others closely related to them remained in Palestine and combined with them again after the return from Egypt. The tribes in the far north, Zebulun, Asher and Naphthali, and those in the south, Judah and Simeon, have traditions about how they came to be there which are different from those of the returning group which settled in the middle part of the country after they came in via Jericho (Judg. 1 and Josh. 15–19). Asher is mentioned as being in Palestine during the reign of Seti I (1309–1290 B.C.) and the victory inscription of Merenptah (1224–1216 B.C.) records the defeat of Israel as well as other peoples in Palestine. It is not clear whether these tribes formed part of an original unified group or whether their unity belonged in reality only to the period after the conquest and settlement.

## Settling in Canaan

As Moses is the hero of the coming out of Egypt, so Joshua is the hero of the coming into Canaan. It is a strong biblical tradition that, when they had crossed the Jordan, Jericho fell to the tribes led by Joshua. The date of this remains uncertain because the remains of the Late Bronze Age city have been almost completely washed away (see pp. 52–3). In the first twelve chapters of the book of Joshua there is an account of a very successful military campaign led by Joshua in command of a large combined force of Israelite tribes. The general tone of these chapters is set at the beginning: 'it is for you to cross the Jordan, you and this whole people of Israel...Every place where you set foot is yours' (Josh. 1: 2, 3). Yet even in these chapters some episodes tell of set-backs, as for example at Ai (Josh. 7: 2–9) and the later chapters give a very different general impression: 'When the Israelites grew stronger, they put the Canaanites to forced labour, but they did not drive them out' (Josh. 17: 13).

Much of the population of Canaan was concentrated in cities and many of these were well defended against intruders. The south, the centre and the north can be seen as separate units but even within these major areas authority was split up between many local kings who owed some allegiance to an overlord such as the king of Jerusalem in the south (Josh. 10: 3) or the king of Hazor in the north (Josh. 11: 1–3). The lack of unity amongst the people already established in Canaan may be partly because of the geography of Palestine and partly because different groups preserved their own identities as far as possible. The Canaanites were for these reasons vulnerable just as in later centuries the Israelites were vulnerable partly because they could not mount a strong enough defence of the whole area against invaders from south and north.

Israelites gained a foothold in the centre, in the south and in the north, but the tribes of the south were separated from those of the centre by the stronghold of Jerusalem, which remained in Jebusite control until the time of David, and the most northerly tribes were cut off because Canaanites held the plain of Jezreel and the Carmel ridge. In many places the Israelite foothold may have been precarious and they would not be in full control of the areas where they were able to settle but still subject to the old local overlords. In such a confused situation as this it is not surprising that no records of any kind have survived. Even if the biblical descriptions of the destructions of cities are somewhat exaggerated the evidence of archaeology does suggest that buildings were flattened, either when they were destroyed or afterwards to clear the site for new fortifications, and even if there were any annals in any of these places none have been found to throw light on this period.

In the biblical traditions, however, much edited before they reach us, there survive stories of Israelite heroes. These 'judges', as they are called, were leaders of tribes or groups of tribes who successfully defended or extended Israelite territory here and there. Although the tribes were not yet all united in any political sense these exploits probably helped to strengthen the sense of identity and to foster the unity which derives from common ancestry and common religion. Tribes from the north and centre did combine in battle against Canaanites for possession of the valley of Jezreel (Esdraelon) and this victory was probably important in strengthening the practical unity between these two Israelite groups as well as giving them control over an important territory (Judg. 4 and 5). From others of these stories it is clear that Israelites had to contend not only against Canaanites but against other tribes coming in from the desert.

The greatest danger threatened, however, from the west when the Philistines settled on the coast. Rameses III had eventually repulsed them from Egypt which they had threatened between 1170 and 1165 B.C. They settled in the five city-states, Ashdod, Gaza, Ashkelon, Gath and Ekron. Samson had some success against them but they nevertheless forced the tribe of Dan to migrate from the western foothills to the slopes of mount Hermon in the north. The Philistines were better armed and better organized and the Israelites were obliged to combine into a larger unit if they were to maintain the position they had achieved. Combining into a larger unit meant having a leader of the larger unit, one with a higher status than that of a tribal chief. This was not the first time that the question had arisen, but Gideon had refused the kind of rulership which involved a succession from father to son (Judg. 8: 22) and when the half-Canaanite Abimelech had set himself up as king (Judg. 9) he had been rejected.

It seems to have been the prophet Samuel, whose headquarters were first at Shiloh and later at Ramah, who put forward Saul as the man who should be chosen to lead a combined force of Israelites against the Philistine threat. The traditions which have come down to us suggest that tribes less immediately threatened than others came to the assistance of their kin in emergency, though this did not commit them to continue such a close association once the emergency was past. With this kind of help and support Saul had some success at the beginning of his campaign but he failed to establish the Israelite position securely and himself met his death in battle on mount Gilboa which overlooks the plain of Esdraelon some 50 miles from his small fortress–palace at Gibeah, just north of Jerusalem.

Saul was a Benjamite, a member of one of the central block of tribes, but it was David, of the tribe of Judah, who had at one time served under Saul, who stepped into the position of leadership after Saul's death. Stories about David's prowess suggest that Saul was jealous of David even as a young man and that David had to withdraw to preserve his life. Tribes in the north set up Ishbosheth, Saul's son, as their leader, but they could not sustain this position and eventually they became part of the larger grouping which David established from about 1000 B.C.

The traditions about the coming into Canaan and settling there, about the successes and failures of various tribes and groups of tribes, grew together in later years as the tribes themselves later grew more closely together.

## Kings in Israel

David was not only a successful general but a shrewd politician and he managed to secure the loyalty of all the groups of the tribes of Israel. To begin with he operated from his old headquarters in Hebron in Judah but this was not well-placed as a centre for the task he had in mind. The city of Jerusalem was still occupied by the Jebusites and still a threat to anyone else in the area. David captured it and so at the same time removed a threat, inherited the advantages of its commanding position and moved his headquarters to a place without associations which could suggest that he favoured the south more than any other of the Israelite tribes.

The name of the city is evidently connected with the name of a god of the Canaanites called Shalem, which means 'peace' or 'welfare'. David did not change the name of the city, nor did he exterminate or expel its inhabitants. The priest Zadok, who is mentioned as a member of David's entourage, may well have been a leading priest of the Jebusites and he is coupled with Abiathar, the Israelite priest who had been with David in his earlier days. If this is a true interpretation of the inclusion of Zadok it is a good illustration of David's method of bringing together groups of people who traditionally would remain apart from one another. For David had some success in uniting not only the different groups of the Israelite tribes but also Israelites and Canaanites.

David's policies were not welcomed by all Israelites and Absalom's revolt may have been in protest against new developments. It was based on Hebron, which had been David's original headquarters, and we are told that Absalom 'stole the affections of the Israelites' (2 Sam. 15: 6); the hostages which he took from Jerusalem may well have been Jebusites. Absalom was one of David's many sons; for David had made many diplomatic marriages (2 Sam. 3: 2–5; 5: 13–16) to further his political aspirations. Unfortunately the wives and their sons had ambitions too and these led to domestic and national difficulties. Most of David's difficulties within his kingdom were caused by the friction and jealousy which grew up amongst the half-brothers, particularly at the end of the reign when there was much speculation and plotting about who should succeed to the kingship.

During his reign David had been fortunate in that the two great world powers of that time, Egypt and Assyria, had been too much occupied with internal affairs to be looking towards one another. So Palestine, through which either of them must pass to reach the other, and which was so often in the battle line when they were aiming to expand, was left in peace while David was consolidating his position. He overcame the Philistine threat from the west and also defeated the Ammonites on the east. Some of the other smaller states were also conquered and in the north the border was made more secure by an alliance with the Phoenicians.

So long as this state of affairs was maintained there was one ruler over a larger area of Palestine than there had been for some time. David kept this varied collection together, but the underlying differences remained. No greater power attacked so there was no occasion for the testing and possible strengthening of the bond which might have happened in the face of a common enemy. In world terms this was still a relatively small kingdom, but later Israelites saw an idealized version of it as the pattern for a great future Israelite kingdom under a Davidic ruler.

Solomon, after intrigues both before and after his father's death, became king and retained control over his father's kingdom, even slightly extended it. His particular policy was to build a monarchy on the Egyptian model. This meant central control, uniformity of treatment for all, a tax system and foreign alliances. The country, or perhaps the king, prospered financially under this régime and royal buildings, including a temple, were erected in Jerusalem. But the central control was irksome to the main body of the tribes and after Solomon's death his son Rehoboam failed to hold them together. Enough of the centralizing tendency had been absorbed to keep the main body together as one kingdom; so all but the most southerly element remained as the kingdom of Israel, ruled by a king and having a capital city of its own. The much smaller and poorer kingdom of Judah retained Jerusalem as its capital city and it survived until 586 B.C., boasting an almost unbroken Davidic dynasty of kings.

The larger, more northerly, kingdom of Israel was never free of the divisions and rivalries of the groups of which it was made up, and no long-continuing dynasty was established. The country survived as an independent kingdom until Samaria, the capital city which Omri and Ahab had built, fell to the invading Assyrians in 722 B.C. Although Israel in the north and Judah in the south were separated politically, the traditions which they held in common were important to both of them. These traditions were strong enough to make the people feel that they were related to one another and, even when only the small territory round Jerusalem retained any semblance of independence, hopes for the future were for a restored Israel on the Davidic scale.

Israel and Judah and the other small kingdoms in Palestine coexisted for the most part in reasonable harmony. Sometimes one or another made a bid for supremacy and this danger always in the background hampered progress to stable peace and prosperity. But much graver dangers threatened the whole of Palestine from further afield.

## The great powers

David and Solomon had been able to develop their plans relatively unhampered because in the north-east there was a shift of power and the rising new empire of Assyria had not yet embarked on the main phase of its westward aggression. Egypt did not have expanding territorial ambitions though she had retained some control over Palestine, and Solomon had marriage alliances with her.

The period of the Israelite monarchies saw the greatest westward expansion of the Assyrian empire. Its army was temporarily checked at the battle of Qarqar (Karkar) in 853 B.C. by a coalition of Syrian and Palestinian states, in which Ahab led the Israelite forces. But in 735 B.C. Ahaz of Judah refused to join forces with Pekah of Israel and Rezin of Damascus against the Assyrians: he voluntarily paid tribute to Tiglath Pileser III. Damascus was devastated by Tiglath Pileser in 732 B.C.: Samaria fell ten years later.

The Assyrian method of insuring against rebellion in conquered countries was to break up nations and tribes by transporting sections of the population from one place to another; many of the inhabitants of northern Israel were taken away to northern and eastern Mesopotamia and into the land of Israel came deportees from other lands (2 Kings 17: 24). The former land of Israel was administered as a number of Assyrian districts, including Samerina, which was the new name for the central area of the country. Politically speaking Israel of the north and Judah of the south were now more apart than before but the bond of a common religion was not broken and we are told that Yahweh was worshipped still in the north (2 Kings 17: 41). The traditions that have come down to us in the Old Testament have been handed down by southern compilers and have been heavily influenced by the Jerusalem-centred point of view which, as time went on, condemned more and more severely all worship that had been offered elsewhere. Eventually the Jews of Jerusalem dissociated themselves entirely from the religious group called the 'Samaritans'. The Samaritans claimed to be faithful to an ancient, perhaps even a pre-Jerusalem, tradition; their descendants are still living at Nablus (see p. 59). Because Samaritans and Jews give different reasons for the breach between them we cannot be certain either when or precisely why it became final.

After the fall of Samaria Ahaz of Judah carried on his subservient policy, but his son Hezekiah decided to make a bid for independence. Sargon II died in 705 B.C. and Hezekiah and other rulers in Syria and Palestine judged that the time was ripe for revolt. But although Sennacherib did have problems at home and on other frontiers, he moved west against the revolt and in 701 B.C. he annexed Judaean towns and took many prisoners. Although Jerusalem remained intact Sennacherib claimed heavy tribute and on all counts Judah was the poorer for this attempt to break away from the Assyrian yoke. Hezekiah's son Manasseh, who reigned for the unusually long period 687 to 643 B.C., had no choice but to accept the position and make the best of it; but Josiah who succeeded as king after the brief reign of Amon was able to make another bid for freedom.

The biblical accounts of the reigns of Hezekiah and Josiah are much concerned with the concentration in those reigns on the worship of Yahweh alone in Jerusalem. These writers commend the abolition of other gods from the temple and all traces of the ways in which they were worshipped. The kingdoms had been established in places where Canaanites had practised Canaanite cults and many Canaanites remained, and the populations and their religions had coalesced to some extent. But there seems always to have been a party particularly loyal to Yahweh which held that no accommodation should be made to other peoples, other cultures, other gods. The so-called reform of the Jerusalem cult reflects a situation in which this point of view had gained a hearing; it was associated with a policy of non-engagement with other nations whether by paying tribute to them or by co-operating with them.

Josiah was more fortunate, or more skilful, in the timing of his revolt than Hezekiah had been. Assyria was under attack on its mountainous eastern border from the Medes and Persians and in the south from the Chaldaeans (Babylonians). Nineveh was taken in 612 B.C. and this so alarmed pharaoh Necho of Egypt that he set out for the north leading his army through Palestine with the intention of coming to the aid of his former enemy Assyria. At Megiddo, where the coast route crosses the Carmel range and strikes inland, he was met by Josiah; what actually happened on this occasion is not clear, but Josiah lost his life and this was the end of any hope of real independence for Judah.

Pharaoh Necho pursued his march northwards as far as the Euphrates, but he was defeated in 605 B.C. at the battle of Carchemish. In the following year king Nebuchadnezzar followed up the victory by moving south and collecting tribute from the small kingdoms, including Judah. The events of this period of the Babylonian empire are recorded in the Babylonian Chronicle and from that document we also learn that fighting continued between Babylon and Egypt. This probably encouraged king Jehoiakim to withhold the payment of tribute as a gesture of defiance against his overlord. Jehoiakim died, but Nebuchadnezzar took strong action against Jerusalem, deposed Jehoiachin, Jehoiakim's son, and appointed Zedekiah to be king in his place, no doubt choosing one who might be expected to submit and pay up. This was in 597 B.C. and a few years later, in 586 B.C., there was further trouble in Jerusalem, more severe measures were taken and a governor, with less authority than a king, was appointed. Nebuchadnezzar's policy was to break resistance by selective transportation; not the wholesale exchange of populations but the removal of all élite groups, political, military and religious. With those who were transported far away from Jerusalem were many who believed that Israel should be exclusively loyal to Yahweh.

## Living among the nations

The Babylonians maintained control of their empire, with its wide variety of populations, including many uprooted from their homes, for less than thirty years after the death of Nebuchadnezzar in 562 B.C. But thirty years is a human generation and long enough for important developments, long enough for a new generation of Israelites to have been born and brought up in exile. We know little about the lands which had been devastated by war and can only suppose that the inhabitants eked out a meagre living while they struggled to restore their flocks and their crops and their dwellings. They had been effectively weakened by Assyrian and Babylonian policies.

The deported leaders fared better in their exile and were free to settle down and exploit their skills for their own benefit as well as that of their captors. Those who in the past had been responsible for religious practice, for teaching and cherishing the old traditions and Israelite culture felt an even deeper sense of responsibility when all these had been uprooted. So it was that when new rulers moved in with new policies some Israelites were to be found ready and enthusiastic for resettlement in Jerusalem. But from now on 'Israel' means a world-wide (as the world was then known to them) community of people, rather than a small political unit in Palestine. There were, indeed, Israelites in Palestine; but also in Mesopotamia, in Egypt and in Asia Minor. In modern times world-wide Jewry is once more such a community in the world: it has grown and spread and since A.D. 1947 there has again been a political unit in Palestine with the old name 'Israel'.

Babylonian power fell to the army of Cyrus, leader of the growing kingdom of Persia, who defeated the last Babylonian king in 539 B.C. Cyrus set out to organize the considerable area which now came under his control by sending back parties of nationals to the areas from which their parents had been taken, to re-organize these impoverished communities and re-establish their national identity. This was not political independence, far from it; such authority as was given to the leaders of the parties was derived from Persia and so it remained for the next two centuries.

After the death of Cyrus' son and successor, Cambyses, the empire was shaken by wars about the succession. Palestine was not directly involved and Darius I, a collateral descendant of Cyrus' line, established himself and restored law and order throughout the empire. In the rock face at Behistun, where the main road from Mesopotamia to Persia pierces the mountain barrier, is the great trilingual inscription which he caused to be cut there giving his own somewhat one-sided version of his rise to power. This is the famous find which provided the key to the understanding of cuneiform (wedge-shaped) script (see p. 48 and *Old Testament Illustrations*, pp. 97–9). The Persian empire was of greater extent and much longer duration than its predecessors in the area. The policy of re-establishing local communities with their own traditions but responsible to Persian authority was reasonably successful. There was more peace and greater prosperity than can have been known for many generations, but Persian conflicts with Egypt and with Greece provided an insecure background and probably a heavy burden of taxation on subject peoples.

We have little knowledge of Israelite settlements other

than those in Palestine: we assume that they existed because of what we know about them in later times. But a notable exception is on the southern border of Egypt near Syene, present-day Aswan. On a little island in the Nile at this point ivory and other African produce were traded for Egyptian goods and it was called 'Elephant Place', in Greek *Elephantine* and in Egyptian *Yeb*. It was also a military post guarding the frontier and the garrison was manned by Jewish soldiers who may have been sent there as early as the seventh century, though the earliest of the many Aramaic documents found there is dated in 495 B.C. Some of these documents throw considerable light on the life of a Jewish community outside Palestine and we learn in some detail about their relations with their non-Jewish neighbours. Remarkably enough they had a temple of their own, in which they worshipped not only Yahweh (Yahu) but also two other deities, a goddess named Anath-Bethel and a young male deity called Eshem-Bethel. A divine triad of this type was worshipped in many other ancient cults, certainly in Egypt at Thebes, Memphis and Edfu. This is so contrary to anything we read of in the Old Testament that we are surprised to learn that when their temple was destroyed in rioting between Egyptians and Jews the Elephantine community appealed to their brethren both in Samaria and in Jerusalem for help to rebuild it. That an appeal was made to both Samaria and Jerusalem suggests that no serious breach between Samaritans and Jews had yet taken place. That a temple was replanned outside Jerusalem suggests that the emphasis on a single sanctuary – found especially in Deuteronomy and the books of Kings – was not universally accepted.

## Under Persian rule

A number of parties went to Jerusalem in the first part of the Persian period. Such knowledge as we have of them must be gathered from the books of Ezra and Nehemiah, but it is difficult to get any clear idea of the sequence of events because the compilers, who in any case were writing long afterwards, were interested in the significance of what was happening, not in historical detail. The first parties who went must have been appalled and disheartened by what they found. Plans for a temple-building operation could not effectively be put in hand until the workmen were housed and fed, and the prophet Haggai laments that the temple work has been abandoned. At last, under the leadership of the governor Zerubbabel and the priest Joshua a temple was completed.

Haggai and Zechariah both speak of Zerubbabel in language which suggests that he may have been regarded as a possible saviour and deliverer, the one who would re-establish Jewish independence, the Messiah of the line of David who would found a new Davidic kingdom. After the building of the temple no more is heard of Zerubbabel; this may be just because no more was known about him or at any rate nothing that seemed important to these compilers. But some scholars take this to mean that the Persians got wind of these messianic aspirations and removed Zerubbabel from his position. However this may have been, the account of the completion and dedication of the temple suggests much loyalty to Darius; prayers are to be offered there 'for the life of the king' (Ezra 6: 10). Perhaps a fair deduction might be that some were for making the best of Persian generosity and some were only interested in hopes of independence; if this is so, it is an early example of what became a serious issue and cause of division amongst the Jews later on.

From now on for about seventy years we know little of affairs in Jerusalem. We can only infer that there were no major upheavals, at any rate none which affected the building up of the new Jewish community in its new setting. But in 445 B.C. another expedition came in, led by Nehemiah who was cup-bearer to Artaxerxes I at the Persian court in Susa. Hearing from his brother that Jerusalem was once more in a deplorable state he persuaded the king to appoint him as governor (Neh. 5: 14) and with this authority he proceeded to put things on a better footing. He refused any co-operation with Samaria and thus roused the enmity of Sanballat the governor. But in spite of this, and of some reluctance amongst the inhabitants of Jerusalem itself, Nehemiah organized the city's defences and brought in enough people from outlying parts to make up a reasonable population to revive the depleted city. This rescue operation took twelve years and in 433 B.C., when it had been completed, Nehemiah returned to Babylon; we are told that later he came on a second mission and introduced further reforms of a more religious and ritualistic kind (Neh. 13: 6–31).

Ezra came to Jerusalem 'in the seventh year of King Artaxerxes' (Ezra 7: 7). If this was Artaxerxes I the date was 458 B.C., in which case he came before Nehemiah. If the king was Artaxerxes II Ezra came in 397 B.C. Three, and only three, verses (Neh. 8: 9; 12: 26, 36) speak of Nehemiah and Ezra together; Nehemiah is a mere onlooker in the first one and so is Ezra in the other two. Perhaps they only appear there together because the much later editor thought that their periods of office overlapped. But it is very difficult to make sense of their work unless Nehemiah was the earlier and so it is very generally supposed that the Artaxerxes in question is the second king of that name.

Ezra's title is given as 'priest and scribe learned in the law of the God of heaven' (Ezra 7: 12): this may be an official phrase meaning something like 'commissioner for religious affairs' and if this was the authority with which he was sent it suggests that it was thought the time was ripe to send one of priestly family to regulate religious affairs. The first thing we are told about him is that he published to the community at Jerusalem the sacred Torah which was henceforth, with the agreement of the Persian authorities, to be normative and to be enforced. Whether this Torah, as put forward at that time by Ezra, was the whole of the books of Moses as we have them in the Old Testament, or only some part of it, we cannot tell. Whatever it was it involved an extensive teaching programme and much work for many learned scribes. Although we know nothing of the details we observe the results later on. With the acceptance of the Torah, and even more with the growing acceptance of its authoritative interpretations, the life of the people was now regulated by a written constitution governing every aspect of life. We only hear of Ezra's work from declared Torah devotees and it may be that others were less enthusiastic, but the Torah expressed Israel's faith in a form in which it survived for centuries without the support of political self-determination, a national home-land or a legally binding authority.

Few details are available for the remainder of the Persian period. There came a time when the high priest was also the governor of the sub-province and minted coinage and collected taxes. But eventually the great Persian empire, one of the most enlightened of all time, declined and fell and new masters arrived in Palestine in 334 B.C.

## The hellenistic kingdoms

The new great power was Macedon. Philip II had conquered Greece, and his son Alexander the Great conquered the Persian empire and Egypt. When Alexander defeated the last Persian emperor, Darius III, at Granicus (334 B.C.), then at Issus (333 B.C.) and finally at Gaugamela (331 B.C.), a new chapter began in the history of the Near and Middle East. Greek influence became paramount; Greek settlers built new cities, Greek customs were adopted and the Greek language became more and more widely known and used. These were probably the most revolutionary changes that had overtaken this part of the world. Babylonia, Assyria and Persia had all had different policies but their cultures had more common characteristics than differences. Alexander initiated sweeping changes and although he did not live long to pursue them his successors carried on the policy of deliberate hellenization, the bringing of Greek culture to peoples who were not themselves Greek, or Hellenic.

When Alexander died in 323 B.C. his generals retained power over the areas where they found themselves when the news reached them. Palestine was annexed by general Ptolemy, who made himself the new master of Egypt, and although it changed hands a number of times because it was on the boundary of his area, he and his successors were usually in control until 198 B.C. The high priest remained both civil and religious head of the community and the Jews were allowed in the main to run their domestic affairs without interference so long as they paid their taxes. Under these conditions the high-priestly class became a kind of ruling group more interested in civil than in religious affairs.

In 223 B.C. Antiochus III, the Great, came to the throne in Syria. He was a descendant of Seleucus, the general who had taken over Alexander's eastern provinces. By now this Seleucid kingdom had two capital cities, one in Babylon and one at Antioch on the Orontes. In 198 B.C. Antiochus managed to seize control of Palestine and thus push his frontier further south and further away from his capital at Antioch. For a time things went on as before in Palestine, indeed the Jewish historian Josephus says that the change was welcomed and that at first Antiochus treated the Jews generously. But he had dreams of expanding his empire westwards and this brought him into conflict with the Romans who by now were taking a great interest in the eastern end of the Mediterranean, a sea which they were beginning to regard as their own. In 190 B.C. Antiochus was defeated by the Romans at Magnesia in Asia Minor and as part of the peace terms he not only had to give up his conquests in Asia Minor but also to pay an enormous reparations bill. This huge drain on his resources led not only Antiochus but also his successors to make more and more financial demands on their subject peoples.

During the first decades of the new hellenizing period sharp divisions had developed amongst the Jews. The issue at stake was whether it was allowable at all, and if so to what degree, to submit to hellenization and to co-operate with the new ruling power: some maintained that there must be complete separation to preserve a corporate purity. Those who were responsible for government knew that the life of the people could only be maintained on the basis of a compromise and for this they were bitterly criticized by those who saw this as unfaithfulness to the Law. The Seleucid kings naturally wanted friendly high priests on whom they could rely, and there came a time when a Joshua, who actually preferred to be called by his Greek name Jason, offered Antiochus money for the high priesthood and his brother Onias III, the legitimate holder, was deposed. Worse still, a non-priest, Menelaus, bid a higher price and Onias was assassinated, so bitter were the rivalries and factions within the state.

Antiochus IV, Epiphanes, angered by the tenacity with which the people of Jerusalem defended their special position, decided to annul all the privileges of worship and religious observance which his predecessors had allowed. His harsh measures forbade the regular sacrifices, the observance of the sabbath, the rite of circumcision; even to possess a copy of the scriptures was forbidden on pain of death. The temple itself was desecrated by the introduction of an image of Zeus and a pig was sacrificed on the altar. Not all Jews opposed Antiochus; many of them welcomed changes which would replace customs which they themselves thought were out of date. These Jews did not want to be different from other people; they wanted to enjoy the sports and games of the Greeks, to speak an international language and to have access to the rich literary and dramatic tradition. But their opponents believed that the traditional faith enshrined, even in details already archaic at that time, God's eternal and only revelation of his way. This tradition they considered themselves bound to maintain without compromise even at the cost of torture and merciless persecution.

So the unfortunate inhabitants of Jerusalem were caught up in two conflicts. They were caught between the ambitions of the Ptolemaic kingdom in the south and the Seleucid kingdom in the north; as the Seleucid kingdom began to weaken, it too was divided and torn. At the same time they were caught in their own internal conflict between those who were on the whole happy to be absorbed into a wider world and those who were for freedom, particularly religious freedom, at all costs. But it was outside Jerusalem, in the village of Modin, near Lydda, that the strangling cord finally snapped. Here as elsewhere the order had been given that sacrifice be offered to the gods. But Mattathias, a member of the priestly line who happened to live in the village, refused to carry out the order. A neighbour stepped forward to take his place but Mattathias in a rage killed both officer and neighbour. He then fled to the hills with his five sons, John, Simon, Judas, Eleazar and Jonathan, and many other supporters (1 Macc. 2: 1 – 28).

Palestine is geographically well suited to guerrilla warfare, and for some time Judas, and later Jonathan and Simon, carried on a not unsuccessful campaign against the Seleucids, whose own affairs were increasingly difficult and left them less and less time for combating such threats. Judas, commonly known by the nickname 'Maccabaeus', 'the hammer' or perhaps 'the designated one', was strong enough to enter Jerusalem on his own terms, to re-establish the temple and its worship and to satisfy the hopes of those Jews whose only concern was that this, and all that went with it, should be restored to them. Others, however, including not unnaturally the leaders, decided to make a bid for political freedom. The campaign was carried on, and after Judas was killed in battle his brother Jonathan became the leader and carried on guerrilla skirmishing without any great success until king Demetrius I, Soter, was threatened by a pretender to his throne, Alexander Balas. In this extremity Demetrius offered Jonathan independence and Alexander offered him the high-priesthood. Jonathan accepted both offers, though his family was not in the high-priestly group. Although more generally known as Maccabaeans or Maccabees because of Judas' nickname, their family name was Hashmon and they are also known as Hasmonaeans, particularly since they established themselves as a line of Jewish rulers.

Jonathan's brother Simon was allowed to establish an independent Jewish state and reign as high priest, with almost complete freedom from interference, from 142 to 134 B.C. A number of members of this family ruled in succession and strengthened their position. So weak had the Seleucid control become that they were even able to extend their sphere northwards into Galilee which had not previously been under Jewish influence. At the turn of the century the king, as he was now called, was Alexander Jannaeus and he ruled from 103 to 77 B.C. But by now, sixty years after the restoration of the temple and Jewish practices in Jerusalem, the stricter religious party, to whom the name Pharisee is applied and who stood for the application of the Torah to every detail of life, had grown into a serious and influential opposition: they even tried to use force against Jannaeus but he quickly suppressed their revolt and eight hundred of them were crucified in reprisal. This savage affair shows how deep were the divisions which had developed amongst the Jews during the time that they had been free enough to concentrate on their own affairs. Jannaeus' widow, Alexandra, maintained control over his quite extensive kingdom after his death but when her two sons quarrelled with one another the end of Hasmonaean power was in sight.

## Roman occupation

The Roman general, Pompey, was campaigning in Pontus and Armenia at this time and the Hasmonaean brothers appealed to him for support and judgement. This brought the new and well-organized power of Rome into Palestine, and after yet another period of confusion and blood-shed order was restored once more, though Jewish independence was at an end. Judaea was organized as a Roman province and all the various parties amongst the Jews had to adjust themselves yet again to a new situation.

Again, though within a shorter time, the appointed rulers, the Herod family, only part-Jewish, were successful to begin with in restoring order and prosperity and later in threatening the occupying power. Again, too, a strong frontier position encouraged patriots to revolt in a bid for freedom but this time without any success. The Romans had to come in force, first led by Vespasian and later by Titus who eventually subdued Jerusalem in A.D. 70. Even this severe defeat did not extinguish all Jewish hopes and new resistance was led by Simon bar Kosiba (Bar Cochba) until A.D. 135 when the Romans finally quelled it. At this time they rebuilt Jerusalem as an entirely non-Jewish city and renamed it Aelia Capitolina.

During these last years the Jewish community lived in an atmosphere of much religious as well as political uncertainty. Christianity was growing and spreading and

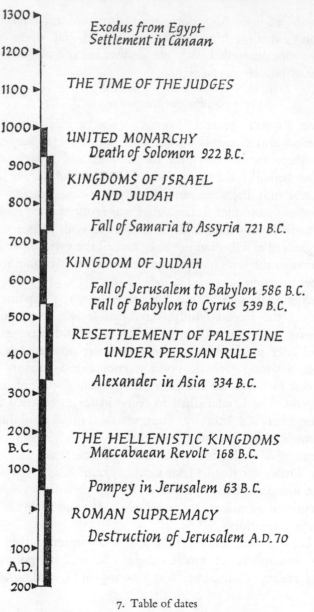

1300 ►
   *Exodus from Egypt*
   *Settlement in Canaan*
1200 ►

1100 ►   *THE TIME OF THE JUDGES*

1000►

   *UNITED MONARCHY*
     *Death of Solomon  922 B.C.*
900►

   *KINGDOMS OF ISRAEL*
     *AND JUDAH*
800►

   *Fall of Samaria to Assyria 721 B.C.*
700 ►

   *KINGDOM OF JUDAH*
600►

   *Fall of Jerusalem to Babylon 586 B.C.*
   *Fall of Babylon to Cyrus  539 B.C.*
500 ►

   *RESETTLEMENT OF PALESTINE*
400►     *UNDER PERSIAN RULE*

   *Alexander in Asia  334 B.C.*
300 ►

200►
B.C.   *THE HELLENISTIC KINGDOMS*
   *Maccabaean Revolt  168 B.C.*
100 ►

   *Pompey in Jerusalem 63 B.C.*
►
   *ROMAN SUPREMACY*
   *Destruction of Jerusalem A.D. 70*

100►
A.D.
200►

7. Table of dates

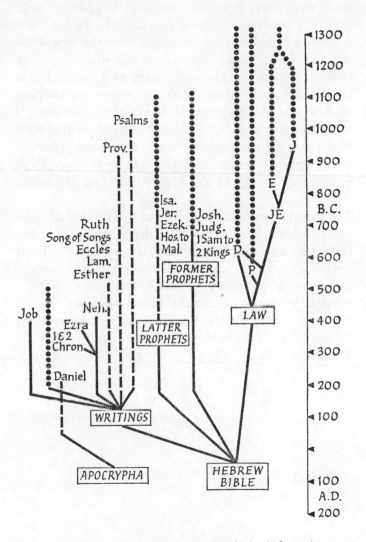

8. Books of the Old Testament. (For further information
see *Old Testament Illustrations*, p. 137)

there were many different groupings in Judaism itself. All these pressures made it necessary to find a clear definition of Judaism which would meet the new situation. So far as books were concerned there was close consideration of which books were to be regarded as sacred, and great attention to the precise preservation of their text. To preserve the life of the community it was essential to maintain absolute loyalty to the traditions of the past and the books in which these were preserved were of primary importance. (For a fuller account of this process see chapter 4 of *The Making of the Old Testament*.)

The long history which lies behind this time of decision and definition has provided on the whole an obscure, frequently a violent, background: less is known of times which were more peaceful. Within this great variety and through the many violent changes there grew a religion whose story can be pieced together, not at every point very clearly, but finally very convincingly, by careful and informed study of the books of the Old Testament itself.

# 3

## THE HISTORY OF RELIGION
## IN ISRAEL

### IDEAS AND BELIEFS IN THE BACKGROUND
### OF THE OLD TESTAMENT

The first step towards understanding the Old Testament and the Apocrypha is to find out, if possible, when and why they came to be written. Fortunately for us this is now possible: there are still different opinions about many of the details and their interpretation, but there is general agreement about the main stages of the story. It is well understood that the books were not 'written' in the sense that an author sets out to 'write' a text book or a novel or a play or a piece of poetry. The books include sections deliberately composed to be recited or read, but this does not apply to whole books, still less to the Old Testament as a whole, or to the Apocrypha.

The second step is to find out as much as we can about the background story of ideas which are older than the ones we find in the Old Testament itself. Although the Old Testament opens with stories about the beginnings of things, many thousands of years of human development had passed before these stories even began to be made. Archaeological studies show very clearly that the religious beliefs of men in ancient times were very varied. The idea that there was some starting point which can be recognized and then a straightforward growth and development from that, each stage clearly related to what went before, is not supported by the evidence. Even if we are studying only one part of the world this is not what the evidence suggests and when we compare the results of work in different parts of the world the varieties are even more in number. Different families of ideas which we can now study and describe lived on and developed in different places. When groups of tribes moved about and found new neighbours, they influenced one another. Everywhere and all the time habits and customs and ideas were affected by the environment and the social and political circumstances of tribes and nations and empires, just as they are nowadays.

The study of ancient documents, particularly books, shows how the actual writing down of traditions affects the traditions themselves. For many generations beliefs and codes of behaviour were passed on by word of mouth, parents teaching children and wise men guarding the truth of the corporate inheritance of the community. But once these traditions had been written down, the actual written statements, whether on stone, or clay tablets, or whatever material, began to have an authority of their own. Teaching what had been written down still had to be done by word of mouth, for very few could read, but there was a new factor of authority: the writing that lies behind what is taught; and this may make the tradition less flexible than it once was.

Although old ideas may live on in the sense that they are in the background of customs and practices which originally depended upon them, the ideas in their explicit form may disappear. The ideas will die out if they cannot help men to make the adjustments that are called for as the circumstances of life change. If the ideas have once been written down, however, they may survive in written form even if they are not relevant to man's new needs; they will only disappear if the documents are all destroyed or completely lost. In the written documents which survive, newer ideas take their place alongside the older ones and this is why not only variations but even contradictions are found. The Old Testament is a large collection of such material; it covers a number of periods of change and it has never been stream-lined.

If mankind had reached an agreed and universally accepted set of beliefs and customs, the history of past efforts would be only of interest to specialists. But mankind is very far from such a state of affairs and most of us cannot imagine what it would be like. We are acutely aware of cultural and religious differences and the conflicts which they breed. In our search for more successful ways of living together and organizing human relationships we take into account our own circumstances and try to understand them. Because the problems are so complex and so far from being solved it is worth while looking at other efforts, in different places and at different times, to come to terms with human problems. For it is reasonably certain that in the twentieth century people are holding on to some old ideas which are no longer serviceable, without even knowing it. Looking back we can see that this is what the old Israelites were sometimes doing; to observe them and their ways of reform may help us to be more critical of ourselves.

## Man and his environment

Evidence of many different kinds suggests that man's first wonderings and questionings have been about himself, his identity and his relationships with other human beings and with the rest of his environment. In the natural, visible world there are animals and plants and the weather, and movements and changes which happen for no obvious reasons. For example, water flows, trees move, storms rise. Sometimes people have felt that trees and streams are like human beings, that they have personality which expresses itself by choice and will, like human personality. But this has never been a popular idea; human beings feel deeply that they are different, even from other animals. It has been much more usual to suppose that there are other forces in the environment which are not visible. Some of these may be invisible beings with powers something like animal and human powers and for such beings the words 'spirit', 'god' and 'demon' still survive in our languages. The ideas that they stand for also survive in many different meanings in most cultures: but these same ideas have also been completely rejected by large numbers of people in the modern world. What has been rejected is the old interpretation of external forces in terms of beings behaving like persons. When the words are still used they come in phrases like 'the spirit of the age', 'the fighting spirit', where the word has no personal meaning at all.

When the existence of invisible forces and beings is accepted as the explanation of things which cannot be explained any other way, the urgent next question is: what are the relationships between men and these spirits? If they are like the relationships between human beings perhaps there can be communication between men and gods. Questions of this kind had already been asked long before there was any writing; then answers had been suggested and experience led on to further questions.

## Questions about man

As soon as he begins to think or reflect at all, man is aware that his experience is with other people, with other animals, with the natural world. He may think, too, about himself as an individual and be conscious of feelings and powers and the necessity to choose between one thing and another. Not very many individual human beings are articulate about this kind of thing at any time, but those who are lead others, and eventually whole societies come to hold common beliefs which have at first been the thoughts of a few. Artists, inventors, rulers and teachers all shape history by the effect they have on the rest of us. Once upon a time wheels first came into use as machines; can we imagine life without them? Once upon a time men began to ask 'What is the purpose of living?'; can we imagine a time before that question had been asked, or even a time before it had already been answered in more ways than one? Perhaps the ability to reflect and interpret is one of the most important factors in the description of man as man. In some societies the philosopher is highly regarded, though he soon falls into disrepute if he claims only to answer old questions and does not give expression to new ones.

### (a) Strength and weakness of man

Physically human beings are obviously less strong than, say, tigers and crocodiles. Nor can human beings resist, unaided, many illnesses caused by tiny organisms. Violent weather conditions, storm, flood, drought and earthquake, may destroy tribes and villages, even towns and their populations. In other ways, too, people are aware of weakness and vulnerability. It frequently seems impossible to make any impression on other people, to persuade them to change their ways of behaving. Many changes which some would like to see cannot be brought about even by force. Many people seem to be the victims of circumstances over which they have no control and are acutely conscious of their lack of power.

In spite of all this, the overruling general conviction of man is that he is strong, that he exercises a considerable degree of control over his environment and that this will increase as he understands it better. He can and does learn how to avoid or defend himself against tigers and crocodiles, and he finds some treatments and preventives of disease. He learns how to come to terms with his neighbours and continually hopes to establish peace, possibly through his own domination. Naturally if ways and means of organizing the environment are found to work up to a certain point, there will be hope of further improvement and of the ultimate achievement of full control. This is the general expectation; it is challenged by the less optimistic point of view of a minority who steadily point to man's failures and can only foresee his extinction.

A strong conviction of man's worth, power and responsibility rings through the Old Testament, in spite of much lamentation about his failure to live up to his calling. In the Old Testament this conviction is reinforced and illuminated by the ruling belief in one all-powerful God, the belief which had grown up in Israel by the time the Old Testament books were put together. The Israelite belief is that God has put man in his place on earth to 'be fruitful and increase, fill the earth and subdue it, rule over the fish in the sea, the birds of heaven, and every living thing that moves upon the earth' (Gen.

1 : 28). Israel is exhorted to 'remember the LORD your God; it is he that gives you strength to become prosperous, so fulfilling the covenant guaranteed by oath with your forefathers, as he is doing now' (Deut. 8 : 18). This conviction about strength and prosperity rests on a tradition which was already old when the books were composed.

The honest and thoughtful man recognizes that he is a mixture of strength and weakness; his problem is to know how best to exercise the degree of power and responsibility that he has. Part of his responsibility is to sharpen his judgement about himself, to learn to strike a sound balance between his strengths and his weaknesses. This freedom of decision is another important item in the definition of a human being.

## (b) *Freedom or bondage*

The human family includes a rich variety of types. Besides the specially gifted individuals on whom we depend so much for leading our thinking there are some who are adventurous, some who are more inclined to observe, some who are for action, some who wait to see what others do. These differences affect men's ways of interpreting their environment, and different interpretations mean different beliefs and different attitudes to life. Many believe that new truth is continually being revealed to those who have courage to receive it: others are driven to explore new ground for themselves.

Active study of how things work has brought about the making of machinery, at first very simple, and its use for transport, agriculture, building and domestic organization. So man's special gifts have been used to develop his particular style of living, which has, in its turn, been the springboard for more exploration and new discovery. Some respond more enthusiastically than others to new knowledge and the new skills which develop out of it. There are always many who fear change and resist it.

New knowledge and understanding bring with them new responsibilities and call for new decisions. In new situations tradition does not always provide sufficient guidance and risks have to be taken. The greater man's confidence in the reliability of the environment the greater his confidence in his own judgement and his willingness to respond to new challenges. Leadership has to be forward-looking and enterprising if it is to inspire confidence and lead the whole group to further development and increased understanding.

The way of understanding can be laborious and it is not always successful. The determination to get the better of adverse circumstances can show itself differently, in the search for methods of control which can be learned and passed on from generation to generation without analysing reasons and learning to understand the processes. If this can be done successfully it offers a much simpler alternative. This way depends on the belief that different agencies have different parts to play and that all man need do is to learn his part, remember what is required of him and carry it out. The most efficient method will be to appoint individuals to carry the responsibility of performing the rituals on behalf of the whole community. For example, it will be their responsibility to make sure of rain for the crops by pouring out water at a particular place and time in confidence that the gods will then play their part by pouring rain from the heavens. This is easier than learning how to choose the best places for sowing and devising methods of irrigation to maximize the use of water. But it is no incentive for further development or improvement.

## (c) *Responsibility or refusal*

These two ways of life both depend on supposing that there is some sort of chain of cause and effect: the difference between them is the difference between supposing that man cannot understand how the chain works and supposing that he can set to work to find out with some hope of success. Both aim at control, the one by the performance of rituals, the other by discovering increasingly efficient methods. The two developed side by side without any awareness of the kind of distinction we now make and they were used side by side. There can never be any means of proving which, if either, has brought about success or failure.

In practice the two tend to compete with one another. The clash between the pursuit of understanding and the refinement of other ways of control appears over and over again in cultures which are old enough to be seen in perspective. This clash is one of the most persistent elements in the Old Testament. In spite of professional claims and in spite of general apathy, the insistent call is to understanding and responsibility. The obedience called for is not blind obedience, but obedience in faith. God, who is entitled to the obedience of his people, asks that they shall co-operate with him, not that they shall neglect the gifts that he has given them. He asks that they shall trust him and believe that if men play the human part fully God will continue to reward them and lead them on. 'If only you will now listen to me and keep my covenant, then out of all peoples you shall become my special possession' (Exod. 19: 5).

The life and growth of the people depend on the practice of human skills and arts in the first place; development and prosperity depend upon initiative and experiment. There may be failure due to adverse circumstances or to neglect or inefficiency: but so strong is man's conviction that he *should* live and prosper that when there is failure he seeks for explanations in the hope of preventing any repetition of it.

## (d) *Moral rulings arising from experience*

It is obvious that human beings depend heavily on each other, not only in the relationships of man and wife, parent and child, but within the wider group of kinship, tribe and nation. These relationships are thought of in general as going on naturally, but here too there may be failures and the effort to secure against them produces carefully controlled codes of behaviour. These codes of behaviour are themselves, once they have begun to develop, an important element in the environment. They come to be regarded in the same sort of way as other regularities, such as those of the seasons, and so it is supposed that they too exist independently of man's discovery of them. The relationship of a family or a tribe to possessions is also important and comes to be organized by rules. Property rights must be clearly understood and respected and if they are not observed sanctions will be applied.

When certain methods of caring for flocks have developed and proved themselves it is foolish for any man to disregard them and still hope to get equally good results. Here the penalty is obvious and direct – loss of property and livelihood. Yet there is an element of offence in that this man has set himself up against the rules, the accepted rules of nature. Habits and customs which work out in practice, and they would not have been taken into general use if they did not, begin to take on the character of rules. Anyone who defies these rules is an offender against agreed and established practice; he has defied custom and this is wrong. His offence is against the society whose rule has been broken and if this society believes that its rules have been laid down by its god then the offence is against that god and the penalties may be severe, not only for the individual but for the tribe.

## The wise man

In the context of the Old Testament and the Apocrypha a very high value is placed upon the wise man. Cleverness, efficiency, goodness and obedience all contribute to wisdom but they are not its total. So exalted is the concept of Wisdom that it defies definition except as a great and ever-growing summation of all that is to be desired and hoped for. In the Old Testament the man who is the opposite of wise is called foolish or stupid: this negative, dreary, unconcerned kind of human being is the failure; he is not interested in his fellows and their welfare, nor the world in which he lives. The wise man is lively, concerned, interested and forward-looking; he welcomes responsibility and is confident that reason and good sense will prevail.

Wisdom builds the house,
good judgement makes it secure,
knowledge furnishes the rooms
with all the precious and pleasant things that wealth can buy.

(Prov. 24: 3, 4)

## *Invisible beings*

It has been quite difficult in the latter part of what has been written about man to avoid mentioning the possibility that there may be not only other visible animals but also non-visible beings active in man's environment. This difficulty is really quite instructive because the chances seem to be that this is just how the first ideas of spirits or gods began. The fact that these ideas grew up because certain things could not be explained in any other way does not mean that the ideas are either true or untrue. A guess can be right or wrong and if you know which it is it is not a guess any longer.

The guesses of one generation become part of what later generations take for granted, often never pausing to ask for what we would call evidence. In this way, like practical decisions and moral decisions, ideas come to have an authority in themselves because of custom and because no-one knows what their beginnings were. The movement of water in a stream could be explained by saying that there is a spirit in the stream. As time goes on the spirit of the stream takes on a character and people take it for granted that the invisible spirit is 'real'; they don't ask the original question any more.

It is very important always to remember that nothing in the Old Testament or Apocrypha is old enough to take us back to the earliest questioning days. Practically everywhere it is assumed that spirits good and evil and gods of many kinds are as real as visible human beings and the rest of the natural world. Spirits and gods are not visible, although some of the things that they are believed to have caused can be seen.

There are stories of exceptional occasions when spirits

or gods have been seen; these are generally frightening occasions because they seem to deny the true nature of such beings. Nevertheless these stories reinforce the idea that such beings really do exist and it has been claimed that they prove that the guess is right. But there is no independent evidence either way.

In our documents spirits and gods are taken for granted as part of the scheme of things. For the most part they are defined by the things that they are supposed to do. These actions, such as causing wind and rain, are similar to the things that men can do and they are therefore described in human terms. Such beings are also credited with our personal characteristics of benevolence, malevolence and the like. All such beings are thought of as like human beings because they are described in the terms in which men are described; yet they are different because they do things which men cannot do, or have not yet learned how to do.

## (a) Spirits friendly and unfriendly

Our experience of our environment is mostly neutral; we do not have to stop and think all the time about the movements of the sun, moon and stars or the processes by which we move and eat and sleep. But from time to time the environment seems hostile, as in times of bad weather which adversely affects crops, and this kind of thing can suggest that the spirits are unfriendly, or that they have been offended. Life is not just a series of disasters so there must be some friendly spirits as well and perhaps the two kinds compete and conflict with one another.

If no other explanation can be found it is natural to suppose that the spirits have been offended; gifts may be offered in an attempt to compensate for the unknown offence. Such gifts, either due in advance as a safeguard, or offered afterwards as compensation, can themselves become part of the normal round of rituals; later generations will carry them out as matters of custom, not pausing to wonder why these customs developed. So the element of non-reason is fixed in the behaviour-pattern, the element of obedience to rules whose immediate purpose is known, but not the relation between the method and the objective.

## (b) *Gods greater and less*

We are aware of distinctions in our societies, of age, of ability, of power, of responsibility, so it is not surprising that similar distinctions should be supposed to exist in the spirit world. In the past most tribes and groups believed themselves to be under the special care and patronage of a god who was named and who was their own particular god as they were his particular responsibility. War between tribes was a trial of strength between the gods of the tribes and the gods themselves participated in the conflict. If larger units, nations and empires, grew, so did the power of those gods who survived as the gods of the bigger and more powerful units. 'Did their gods save the nations which my forefathers destroyed, Gozan, Harran, Rezeph, and the people of Beth-eden living in Telassar?' (2 Kings 19: 12). The gods of lesser, subservient peoples were less powerful and in a subsidiary position. The god of the tribe or nation is the god who has laid down and demands obedience to a code of behaviour. In the Old Testament we find Kemosh, the god of the Moabites, and Dagon, worshipped in Philistia. We do not know for certain how the name of Israel's god was pronounced. In the Hebrew text only the consonants YHWH are written. There came a time when it was felt that the name was too sacred to pronounce, so another word, 'Adonai' (my Lord), was spoken instead and the original pronunciation of YHWH was lost. There is a generally held view that the word was originally pronounced Yahweh and this is now commonly used. The traditional 'Jehovah' of the English versions, which is used in a few places in the New English Bible, is the result in English of associating the vowel sounds of Adonai with the consonants YHWH (see *The Making of the Old Testament*, pp. 143-4, 160). Each tribe and nation claimed supremacy for its god as an expression of its own supremacy over neighbours. So Israelites claimed that their Yahweh was supreme, and that however low their fortunes might fall yet he and they would in the long run be vindicated.

## One only God

By the time the various sections of the Old Testament were put together, however, thoughtful Israelites had begun to say something very different. They said that there is only one real and true God. This is a completely revolutionary idea and very few people understood it or its profound and far-reaching implications. But the Israelite religious tradition was cherished by people who had begun to take this as the only possible belief and so all those old traditions are transfigured by it. Not only did they say that there is but one God, they claimed that their ancestors had worshipped him under the name of Yahweh. The so-called gods worshipped by other peoples were dumb idols, figures that men themselves had made.

What use is an idol when its maker has shaped it? –
    it is only an image, a source of lies;
or when the maker trusts what he has made? –
    he is only making dumb idols.
    Woe betide him who says to the wood, 'Wake up',
    to the dead stone, 'Bestir yourself' !
Why, it is firmly encased in gold and silver
    and has no breath in it.
    But the LORD is in his holy temple;
    let all the earth be hushed in his presence.

(Hab. 2: 18–20)

God is the maker of men. He has brought the universe into being and it works according to his design. He is responsible, not only for the environment of man's living but for the very existence of man himself; man is part of what God is planning and making all the time.

God can never be fully understood by man; gods that man has made for himself might be within his grasp, but not so God who has made man and understands him better than he understands himself. Yet man is a thinking animal, and can make some headway in his thinking, and will be partly right and partly wrong in his conclusions. The only available tests are the tests of experience and these cannot be conclusive: they have to be repeated in different circumstances as generations succeed one another. If God cannot be controlled by man the ancient practices which were designed to secure certain things from the gods, almost by force, are quite ludicrously inappropriate. But revolutionary ideas are not quickly accepted, still less are their implications understood, so the old practices continue.

God is independent of man's fears and aspirations, his desires and his hopes. This does not mean that God is not deeply concerned about human affairs. God loves what he is creating, so it is profoundly believed, and he is utterly to be trusted. Not only does God love but he claims the love and trust of men, of Israel in particular.

> The word of the LORD holds true,
>     and all his work endures.
> The LORD loves righteousness and justice,
>     his love unfailing fills the earth. (Ps. 33 : 4, 5)

As the old customs linger on, so do the old characteristics of the old gods: their fickleness and touchiness, their cruelty and unconcern. Although God is not made by man in the sense that an idol is built or in the sense that he is invented to complete man's explanation of his environment, still he can only be described by man in man's own words. So it is that those characteristics which men call virtues are attributed to God. Although God is beyond man's understanding he is intimately concerned in man's affairs and working towards better understanding. This is what many teachers in Israel believed and declared, but most of the people, and frequently their rulers, preferred to trust in the old, familiar ways.

## THE FAR PAST OF THE ISRAELITES – THE BOOKS OF MOSES

Opinions vary about when any individual, or some group of individuals, arrived at the epoch-making idea that there is but one true God. Whenever it was, it did not have the effect of immediately blotting out all previous beliefs, still less the religious practices which depended on the old beliefs. But it did mean that many of the old traditions were re-interpreted and some of them took on new significance and were built into the foundations of the new religion. For example, the conviction that the great forefather Abraham had responded to a call, not just from a tribal god with territorial ambitions, but from God, became one of the foundation beliefs. 'I lift my hand and swear by the LORD, God Most High, creator of heaven and earth' (Gen. 14: 22). But stories about Abraham and others which had been told in the days of the older beliefs were still cherished in their old forms, or only slightly modified. 'When the LORD smelt the soothing odour, he said within himself, "Never again will I curse the ground because of man, however evil his inclinations may be from his youth upwards"' (Gen. 8: 21).

The first five books of the Old Testament (Genesis, Exodus, Leviticus, Numbers, Deuteronomy, also known as the books of Moses) include a whole wealth of traditions belonging to the period up to the end of Moses' life, the moment at which Israel's entry into Canaan is immediately expected. Genesis begins with a number of myths and legends about the beginning of the world and the beginning of mankind who lives within it. There are stories to explain how and why relationships have developed as they have, and evidence for the determination to find some reason for everything. The reason for differences of language is provided by the story of the tower of Babel (Gen. 11: 1–9), to give just one example. The books also show how, over a long period of time, the belief had developed in Israel that God is creator of the universe and that Israel has a special place in that universe and a special relationship with God.

> Truly he loves his people
> and blesses his saints.

They sit at his feet
and receive his instruction,
the law which Moses laid upon us. (Deut. 33: 3, 4)

Before man appears in the story at all God is at work making the universe by the power of his word. In other places God is spoken of as making with his hands; 'Thy hands gave me shape and made me' (Job 10: 8). Obviously neither of these ways of describing God's activity is meant to be taken literally. For man, working with the hands is a normal way of making things, but he does not have power to make by 'saying'. The word of God in the first verses of the Bible is not the speech of conversation, not even of revelation, it is the expression of command. What God says is what happens; there is no distinction between what he says and what he does. All these direct commands are 'obeyed', yet 'obey' is not an appropriate word here because the waters and the sky and the sun and the moon are not free to refuse God's command. Human beings can either decide not even to try to express their beliefs about God because of the inadequacy of human language or they can make use of the language they have, as most of them have always done.

Man, too, comes into being at God's undeniable command. But as soon as he appears Adam (originally just one of the Hebrew words for 'man') is found to be in God's image and likeness. This is how the tradition expresses the conviction about man that Israel had reached, as the result of long generations of experience. Man is not God: he cannot create at will, he cannot secure what he wants by giving orders. But neither is he cattle: he can think and plan and secure some of what he wants by organization and planning, and his experience and understanding lead him on to more efficient ways of living (Ps. 8: 3–6). His most potent characteristic is his conviction that he can not only have some understanding of God's work and purposes but that he can even be in some communication with God. Communication of understanding is most naturally expressed in terms of words; so God 'speaks' to Adam and Adam, unlike the reptiles and the birds, can respond to God and in this sense be defined as 'like' him.

Adam is appointed as God's agent to have control over the animal creation. The tribes and nations of the parts of the world where these stories originated in fact had built their prosperity on the development of flocks and herds of sheep and cattle; they had also learned to grow crops of grain and vegetables and in these ways had prospered. Nevertheless, in the tradition, Adam's most remarkable characteristic, after his ability to be taken into conversation by God, is his freedom to disregard God's commands. In the story these commands are clear and man is deliberately disobedient. Through the centuries philosophers debate about defining what is 'right' and what is 'wrong', about individual and corporate responsibility and whether it makes sense to say that anyone can be ignorant but responsible. In this biblical myth primeval man is presented as having been deliberately disobedient.

The great advantage of this theory is that it provides a background explanation for all mankind's most intractable problems. Adam and Eve are punished by being exiled from the environment where all creatures obey the rules of their existence into one where weeds impede cultivation, wild animals do not recognize man's authority; men and women, brothers, tribes, nations live out of harmony with one another.

The stories which follow the Adam and Eve story –

myths, legends, traditions – purport to explain some aspect of human experience. Most of them offer a reason for some adverse feature of human life and history, for anger, fear, hatred, enmity: many of them are probably much older than the carefully thought-out and arranged creation story which precedes them. But they take their places in the scheme because they have all come to have religious significance as examples of what happens in human affairs when the rules which God is believed to have laid down are not observed. Many of the details of these stories are remains of old tribal legends with the old ideas of gods and spirits; some of them have been partially re-interpreted, like the flood story which now takes an important place in the theological picture. Man can neglect his calling and he does, but God is not defeated. There is a faithful man, Noah, who is preserved to be the beginning of a more faithful people after the main body of sinful man has been destroyed.

This is the pattern of most of the early material. Faithful individuals stand out, either quite independent of any background, like Abraham, or against the background of 'disobedient' society, like Noah and Moses. These are holy men, holy in the sense that they are set apart for this calling, the calling to understand, to respond and to interpret. This calling may be fulfilled in word, in deed, or in both: this holiness is not just moral integrity, though it generally includes it. The gods and spirits of early religion had to be negotiated with and sometimes to be placated. The holy men of early religion were those whose special job it was to act for the tribe in the relations with gods and spirits. The community was very dependent upon the skill and integrity of the holy man and on the soundness of his interpretations. He it was who must remind them of old customs if there was a danger of neglect and he was also the one who must seek guidance on their behalf in new situations. So the holy man tended to become just a specialist like other specialists; he might fulfil his calling well or badly and his original function could easily become obscured. Because he was expected to know what was needed to be known he might well be in trouble if the tribe suffered disaster and his calling as such could then be discredited.

## The patriarchs

The great heroes of the Old Testament are holy men in the full and proper sense of the word. Abraham, Isaac and Jacob are presented as individuals specially called to take a place in the working-out of God's purposes. The legends about them are now handed down as a sequence of stories about father, son and grandson and these mark the beginning of the time when the story of one particular people is to be followed, apart from the general story of mankind. For with the idea of one true God came the idea that the forefathers of Israel had been specially called as the forefathers of a people who would recognize God, would worship only him, would obey his laws and take a special place among the nations of the world. 'All nations on earth shall pray to be blessed as your descendants are blessed, and this because you have obeyed me' (Gen. 22: 18).

Ideas of a nation appointed by God to fulfil a special calling grew out of the experience of a small nation. A small, divided and threatened people known as Israel lived in Palestine and for about four centuries, beginning about 1000 B.C., was ruled by kings. During this period the holy men we know most about were prophets.

Although it is the next section of the Old Testament which is specially concerned with the kingdoms and the prophets we have to take a forward look because the experience of those centuries and the teaching and convictions of those prophets profoundly affected the form in which the stories of the far past took shape and have come down to us. This small nation was made up of various tribes named after twelve tribal ancestors and these were understood to have been the sons of Jacob who in the story is renamed Israel (Gen. 35: 9–12).

With the legends of the patriarchs we have not only settled down to one group of people, we have also begun to concentrate on one country – Canaan. The patriarchs were not rulers of Canaan, it was not 'their' country. The last story we have is of Jacob being obliged to leave it because of famine and to move south to Egypt with his family (Gen. 46). The Israelites who subsequently settled in Canaan and controlled parts of it looked back to a time when their ancestors had passed through it. 'They shall live in the land which I gave my servant Jacob, the land where your fathers lived' (Ezek. 37: 25). As they learned to believe in themselves as a special people of God so they learned to think of their land as specially marked out by God for them to live in and to be the scene of the fuller working-out of his purposes in the future.

In Genesis, then, some of the basic elements of Israel's religion are set forth, expressed in terms of old myths, legends and stories. The old material is used to spell out the claim that God who was worshipped in the land of Israel by the people Israel is the creator of the universe. God has plans which involve the special calling of individuals who have been the ancestors of a people: this whole people has now a special calling to fulfil. These stories also declare beliefs about man and his relations with God, or, rather, about how God works with men. The tradition about all these great figures is that God was with them; not as a permanent visible presence, not interfering at every point, but continually present in the wider, more mysterious, background of living and from time to time making his presence more closely felt. Also he was with them in the sense that he was for them, on their side, associating them with himself in the working-out of his purposes. His purposes were not just being worked out through them as if they were puppets, but with them as human beings, human beings made by him, able to understand at least in part and able to respond or refuse. In these stories we get the impression that these men were chosen for responsibility rather than for privilege and that they were required to fulfil their tasks without being able to see at all clearly what the future might hold.

### Moses and the trek from Egypt

The next four books begin with the appearance of Moses on the scene and end with his disappearance from it. So at first sight it might be thought that the books are entirely concerned with material about his life and times and this is partly true. There is a sequence of narrative, or rather a number of narratives, about the journeys which Israelites took from Egypt to Canaan. As with the patriarchs, so with Moses, there is a call to an individual. But this call is to lead a group on a difficult journey and there is an important new feature in the story, the group itself.

The prophets in the times of the kingdoms refer over and over again to the rescue from Egypt; it is one of their most constant themes. It is a theme about God and how he saved his people from bondage. These same prophets do not mention Moses as being particularly important; in fact they scarcely mention him at all – their subject is God and his mighty acts.

But I have been the LORD your God since your days in Egypt,
　　when you knew no other saviour than me,
　　　　no god but me.
　　I cared for you in the wilderness,
　　in a land of burning heat, as if you were in pasture.
(Hos. 13: 4–6)

In the story the people themselves are almost continuously tiresome, unco-operative and unreliable. 'They grew impatient and spoke against God and Moses. "Why have you brought us up from Egypt", they said, "to die in the desert where there is neither food nor water? We are heartily sick of this miserable fare"' (Num. 21: 5). Nevertheless they arrive within sight of the land of Canaan, the land which they are to occupy and where their descendants will settle. So the scene is set for the establishment of God's people as a nation in the land which had been set apart for them, where their fore-fathers had travelled and where no doubt many of their kin had been ever since.

Centuries later Israelites looked back on the great deliverance and believed fervently that God would again bring them to a new beginning.

Thus says the LORD,
who opened a way in the sea
and a path through mighty waters,

　　　　.　　　.　　　.　　　.　　　.　　　.

Here and now I will do a new thing;
　　this moment it will break from the bud.
　　Can you not perceive it? (Isa. 43: 16, 19)

## Moses and the Law

Tradition has it that God revealed his Law at a special place and time, for Moses to pass on to the people and for them to observe. So Moses' place in the tradition is as the first great example of the holy man whose calling is to speak the word of God to the people of God, the kind of holy man generally called a prophet.

The enormous amount of detail, particularly about forms and methods of worship and about life in villages and towns, seems to be directed far ahead of the life-span of the frightened people left at the bottom of the mountain in the story. But the important thing about it all is that, placed as it is, it has for later generations the authority of Moses. This mass of detailed instructions is not unlike an archaeological site which can be uncovered stage by stage, exposing the history of the social and religious customs of the people for whom these customs have become their way of life. The different strands are not always easy to distinguish because they do not only belong to different times, they also belong to different places and different traditions. The tribes who came together to defend themselves against the Philistines round about 1000 B.C. were kindred but they had their own long-established traditions which had grown up separately. When the Philistine threat was finally thrown off by David, and the tribes settled down more permanently, the various groups naturally carried on their own traditions and these were never completely stream-lined. These long-established traditions were the products of the old religions and include much that seems to bear little, if any, relation to the more basic ideas. Many of the customs and practices are the ones which the prophets attacked for

their unsuitability in relation to God as they believed him
to be.

> For the Israelites shall live many a long day
>> without king or prince,
>> without sacrifice or sacred pillar,
>> without image or household gods;
> but after that they will again seek
> the LORD their God and David their king,
> and turn anxiously to the LORD for his bounty in days to
>> come. (Hos. 3: 4, 5)

The prophets seem to have made little headway in their
own time. They criticized the cult because it was so
heavily concentrated on ensuring the assistance of supernatural powers in the old sense. The prophets were
beginning to realize and to preach that God requires a
whole-hearted response from his people in obedience to
their calling, not just in the details of ritual worship but
in every detail of living. The old cult continued nevertheless and its provisions are enshrined in the books of
Moses, re-interpreted but generally preserved in their
original form. The old customs were observed because
they were familiar and old: to question them was to
undermine the very fabric of society. But some reformers
made use of the old material by re-interpreting it and
associating it with what they believed to be particularly
Israelite. So it has come about that the ancient feast of
Passover was newly interpreted to teach the story about
the great deliverance from Egypt; indeed this was done
in more than one way and we have got two examples of
how it was done (Exod. 12: 1–27, Deut. 16: 1–8). Many
of the other observances and rules lack explanation and
must be followed blindly. They seem to lack point

because they call for no response or participation from the people. The re-interpretation of the Passover, which was a corporate observance already (Lev. 23: 5–8), calls for full participation by people who understand the meaning of what they are doing.

When Israelites began to settle in Canaan they found many of the local social and religious customs different from their own. The most obvious reason for this was that the needs and problems of a settled society are in many ways different from those of tribes that are travelling. The patterns of life associated with an economy which is mainly agricultural are different from those of an economy which is chiefly pastoral. The new settlers had the problem that all newcomers have. They had to work out a combination of adapting themselves to new conditions and preserving those customs which they themselves regarded as necessary for preserving their own identity and maintaining continuity with their own past.

During the centuries of the kingdoms and the prophets the adaptation process went on. It was different in different places, particularly at different places of worship. Different families of priests left their mark on the customs that developed. Prophets had groups of disciples who followed them in new ways of thinking. By the end of the kingdoms, when the small surviving kingdom of Judah was gravely threatened, a great variety of tradition had accumulated. This body of tradition claimed ancient authority and it may be that some attempt was made, even after the exile from Jerusalem, to organize it into one consistent whole. If any such version did exist it failed to secure general acceptance; the varieties survived and still survive within the context of the Moses stories and with all the authority that comes with them from that far past.

The final threat to any Israelite political independence in Palestine did not undermine the belief that this was the land where God's people were to be established, and on this note the oldest traditions conclude. The older a tradition is the more powerful it becomes, unless it is totally discarded. The Moses material as we have it emphasizes two characteristics of God which were not so conspicuous in relation to the patriarchs. The first is his determination (we have to use human words), in spite of man's slowness, to pursue his plans. The second is his unlimited readiness to forgive. Forgiveness is God's response to man's change of mind from refusal to obedience and recognition of his past disobedience. God does not force even his forgiveness on those who have sinned; he waits for their change of mind, however fitful and half-hearted.

These traditions also illustrate some of the fundamental characteristics of human beings, particularly their un-willingness to change or to listen to leaders who exhort them to think and try out new ways. Tradition can be a vital part of a good environment for development: it can also be a grave handicap when it holds men back from the opportunity to experiment and develop, which is such a large part of the human inheritance and endowment.

## God at work in the far past

With the realization that the oldest traditions have been deeply influenced by the experience of later generations and by their hopes for the future, perhaps a far future, the books about the pre-settlement period can be looked at as a whole. Jews of later generations called them the Law or Teaching: as they stand they include, as laid down from the beginning of Israel's history, what Israel needs to know about her vocation and the terms of its fulfilment.

God is alone in majesty and power. Long before this could be understood, or even glimpsed, by men, he has been working on a plan for bringing the whole world to understand just this. Mankind is made by God in God's own image, free to think and explore: but he is equally free to be timorous and lazy. Israel has been singled out and is being prepared to be the people who will reach understanding. This people will settle in the land that is also called Israel, and become a nation. God's people will be a witness to the whole world; through them all mankind will be blessed.

Israel will witness not only to the true God but also to the way of true life for man. Man is called to respond of his own free will and understanding, not just to conform to set rules like the sun, moon and stars. This means every individual man, not just specially gifted individuals, and all peoples, not just Israel. We now know that the development of life on this planet before man even appeared took an almost unimaginably long time. Many very early ideas about the beginning of history describe it in terms of bringing order out of chaos, arranging things in appropriate relation to one another. The patterns become more and more complex as time goes on; gradually order emerges and this ordering is something which man can observe and learn to understand. But the bringing of order into human relationships seems to lag behind. It remains to be proved whether Israel's claims in this field can be justified. The meticulous observance of the Law by small groups has no doubt been a fruitful exercise for some but it does not seem to have had much effect upon the world at large.

If, looking back from the twentieth century, it seems that the Israelite promise has not yet been fulfilled, this must not inhibit us from appreciating and respecting the hopes which grew out of that belief. The beliefs and the hopes were the fruits of re-interpreting old traditions. Enough remains in the wilderness stories to remind us that those journeys did not at the time seem like the triumphal progress suggested by later phrases about God leading his people out of slavery and bringing them to a rich and prosperous country. Later reflection has seen the migrations as part of the working out of God's plans for the people; this commentary on the tale can be recognized in the actual text.

Later reflection on the codes and customs is less clearly in evidence. The evidence is there, particularly in Deuteronomy and in Leviticus 17–26, but much of the old cult material has been handed down in forms which presuppose the old, not the new, religion. Religious practices are always more tenaciously preserved than others because there is not likely to be any urgent need for change as there may be with social customs. The families of priests who carried on the worship at the local hill-shrines were no more likely than any other professional group to change their ways without overwhelming reason. The challenge of the prophets may seem to later generations an unanswerable one but at the time it was strange and disturbing and the majority were not convinced by it.

Some adjustments were made because of the new conditions of life, particularly the taking over of rituals associated with settled life and agricultural practice. Some of these were adopted wholesale and still related to the gods of the land already in occupation. National pride, as a nation developed, transferred these to Israel's god, but the gods of other nations were still taken into account in the old way. The most important change is the one already mentioned, the association of the regular yearly festivals with the escape from Egypt and the opportunity to develop as a nation like other nations.

As in the wilderness, so in Canaan, the people frequently fail to do what is required of them, deliberately, or by default, or just in ignorance. Making reparation for such errors becomes in itself the basis of a large number of regulations and requirements. Much of this is mechanical routine, some demands a more personal and individual response. All of it goes in as part of the great complex of required behaviour and the system of rewards and punishments. The total system which has been worked out, which is partly like the systems of other peoples and partly special to Israel, is now claimed to be a full and faithful account of what God requires of his people. The claim rests on the tradition that God himself has already revealed these requirements to Moses and that he did so even in advance of the circumstances in which they would apply.

For Moses has won the reputation of being the great prophet to whom God revealed, in great detail, the method by which order would be achieved in Israel's affairs. This covers the ordering of man's relations with his fellow men and the ordering of man's times and places of approach to God. All these traditions were most zealously cherished by religious leaders of the people who were deported from Jerusalem at the end of the sixth century B.C. Away in Babylon they could not carry out the rituals which had been carried out in Jerusalem and in other holy places in Israel. But the instructions could be cherished in written form in readiness for the return to their own land which God must surely be preparing for the future, as he had brought their forefathers out of Egypt in the past. These traditions and instructions grew into the great complex of the Law which is now the first main section of the Bible.

Experience of life in Babylon deepened and strengthened the conviction that Israel's belief is the true belief. Exile brought into renewed significance the tradition of the great salvation of the old tribes from slavery. The obliteration of Israel as a political entity raised deep questions about the possible reasons for the collapse. Whatever the reason for the present eclipse of Israel's fortunes it could only be a matter of time before Israel would be vindicated as God's chosen people and Israel's God as the only God.

But the questions persist. One obvious possible explanation of Israel's failure to survive could be her failure in obedience. There could be no denying that the nation as a whole had not maintained an exclusive loyalty. God could be punishing his people, or it could be that until they recognize only him they cannot take their rightful place. This argument strongly reinforces the importance of the Law, of preserving it, even of developing it further.

Within the Law itself, however, are some exhortations of a very general character which cannot be obeyed like simple commands. Even 'Remember to keep the sabbath day holy' (Exod. 20: 8) has to be explained: how is it kept holy? who decides? Answers can be given to this kind of question, but what about 'You must love the LORD your God with all your heart and soul and strength' (Deut. 6: 5) and 'you shall love your neighbour as a man like yourself' (Lev. 19: 18)? A man may observe

133

the sabbath and all the provisions of this kind of law; he may do so because it is the custom, or because he is afraid of the consequences if he does not, or in loyalty to his upbringing. None of these need have any relation to 'loving God'. What can this mean? How can man love God? This great command marks a climax of insight and it opens up an entirely new way of thinking about man in relation to his creator. A man may not be tempted to remove his neighbour's boundary stone or covet his neighbour's wife. If he does not wrong his neighbour in such ways is he loving his neighbour 'as a man like himself'? This way of describing man's responsibility to man is another great new step towards thinking about society in quite new ways.

These two great commands come down to us surrounded by echoes of a past which seems far off in so many ways. But these sayings are now, as they always have been, contemporary because they go to the root of man's deepest problems, his problem about himself and his identity and his problem about the society in which he finds himself.

### THE MORE RECENT PAST OF THE ISRAELITES – THE BOOKS OF PROPHETS AND THE PSALMS

The stories of the crossing of the Jordan under the leadership of Joshua lead into stories about the earliest settlements. Then follows the establishment of a kingdom, the split into two kingdoms and the defeat of first one and then the other, ending with the fall of Jerusalem in 586 B.C., and its aftermath. The traditions that we have about this period are mostly to be found in books bearing the names of individuals – Joshua, Samuel, Jeremiah,

Hosea and others – or the titles of leaders and rulers –
Judges and Kings.

The events of which these books tell fall within a period
of about 600 years, but none of the books give anything
like a full account, even of the economic and political
happenings of those centuries. They are concerned only
with a selection of events and occasions and the basis
of selection is the religious conviction of those who
believed that Israelites should be exclusively loyal to
their own religion. Such a loyalty would mean that
they would keep aloof from the general beliefs of
other nations about national gods and therefore from the
local political scene. After both the Israelite kingdoms
had been wiped out it was natural that people who took
this point of view should interpret the disasters as a just
punishment for the disloyalties of kings and people
(Zech. 1: 1–6).

The distinctive beliefs of Israel were worked out against
the background of the experience of settling in the land
which is now known as Palestine, making relationships
with those who were already living there, defending
themselves against the threat of Philistine invasion and
establishing a kingdom under the rule of David. Then
came a different kind of experience, for David's kingdom
and its successors were among many small independent
units in the area all of which were ultimately swallowed
up by the much greater powers of Assyria and Babylon,
which invaded their countries from the north.

## Prophets

The books which are concerned with the affairs of this
period are gathered together under the overall title of
'Prophets' because prophets were the distinctive figures

of the time of the two kingdoms, at any rate from the point of view of those who collected the tradition together. Groups of prophets had always been part of the religious set-up in Israel and in neighbouring countries (I Sam. 10: 5), but these were individual teachers and preachers. Some of them are known to us by name because we have the stories about them and what they said; but there may have been many others too. These prophets claim to know what God's will is because he has revealed it to them and they declare it to kings and priests and people. Prophets are frequently in evidence when one or other of the kingdoms is caught up in the affairs of its neighbours and behaving like them. The prophetic claim is that God's command must be obeyed if Israel is to survive, let alone prosper.

A great deal of the prophecy which has been handed down to us is the threat of disaster as punishment. Past events and present dangers are interpreted as God's punishment for past and present disobedience. Disobedience is disloyalty and disloyalty has been shown by worshipping other gods, even by permitting this worship on Israelite soil. Israelites can only truly worship God in ways appropriate to him and these ways do not include all the practices of the earlier occupants of the land.

> They forsook the LORD, their fathers' God who had brought them out of Egypt, and went after other gods, gods of the races among whom they lived; they bowed down before them and provoked the LORD to anger. (Judg. 2: 12)

The prophets did not quote Moses as their authority, but they did presuppose a standard of faith and life belonging to the past.

Listen, you leaders of Jacob, rulers of Israel,
should you not know what is right? (Mic. 3: 1)

Of course we have only a small amount of all that they must have said, but it is hard to believe that they preached Moses when there is no evidence for this in the material we have. There were places of worship, holy places, all over the country, staffed by priests, members of the hereditary priestly families, and there must have been considerable differences from place to place. Frequently the holy place would be the one which was the holy place before Israelites settled. Sometimes it may have been much as it was then, the Israelites having conformed to what they found. They were adjusting themselves to being more settled and learning agriculture, and they adopted the religious customs appropriate to an agricultural economy. Elsewhere Israelites may have become dominant and their pastoral customs and religious practices dominant, but everywhere they would be mixed with other people, in some proportion or other. In the prophetic books there is criticism of those priests who, while claiming to be priests in Israel, practised the customs associated with Baal or some other god.

I brought you into a fruitful land
    to enjoy its fruit and the goodness of it;
    but when you entered upon it you defiled it
    and made the home I gave you loathsome.
The priests no longer asked, 'Where is the LORD?'
Those who handled the law had no thought of me,
    the shepherds of the people rebelled against me;
    the prophets prophesied in the name of Baal
    and followed gods powerless to help. (Jer. 2: 7, 8)

The prophets preached in two directions, as it were. On the one hand they called the people back to the loyalty of the time before the meeting with Canaanites and their gods. On the other hand they tried to urge them forward, to look ahead and think about how to confirm and express their loyalty in new circumstances. Not all the customs of previously settled communities were right for Israel when she in turn became a sizeable state. The most obvious example of this is in the question about whether she should have a king or not. (Compare 1 Sam. 8: 1–10 with 9: 15, 16.) Some believed that God himself was Israel's only king. After David had become king and had captured Jerusalem from the Jebusites and made it his capital city there was a question whether he should build a temple in it or not (2 Sam. 7: 1–7).

Not only for kings and for leaders and teachers but amongst the body of the people, and in their localities, the implications of Israel's belief must be different from the implications of the cults of Baal and local gods. If Israelites settle alongside societies where wide discrepancies between wealth and poverty have developed, they must not follow suit. If these established societies are built on a complexity of relationships including slavery as one of its institutions, it does not necessarily follow that Israel may do the same and buy and sell human beings.

> When a fellow-Hebrew, man or woman, sells himself to you as a slave, he shall serve you for six years and in the seventh year you shall set him free. But when you set him free, do not let him go empty-handed. Give to him lavishly from your flock, from your threshing-floor and your winepress. (Deut. 15: 12–14)

Issues such as these are raised by prophets during the years of the kingdoms. One after another they urge Israel –

king, priests and people – to think carefully whether or not their plans are in harmony with God's revealed will. Frequently the prophet is urging that they are not.

> The LORD speaks thus of this people: They love to stray from my ways, they wander where they will. Therefore he has no more pleasure in them; he remembers their guilt now, and punishes their sins. Then the LORD said to me, Do not pray for the well-being of this people. When they fast, I will not listen to their cry; when they sacrifice whole-offering and grain-offering, I will not accept them.
> (Jer. 14: 10–12)

As the Bible is now arranged, the answers to the questions appear to have been given beforehand, in the books associated with Moses. But, as we have already seen, they are rules which were worked out and gathered together over a long spell of time. When the prophets recall earlier times they are thinking that there were times when Israel had but one loyalty and the people followed the prophetic lead. The tradition that we have does not really suggest that the tribes *were* always faithful and obedient, though it does suggest that they did turn to better ways when strongly exhorted to do so and that when they listened and obeyed their affairs prospered.

## (a) *Prophets as innovators*

So the prophets of the kingdoms stand not only as traditionalists but also as innovators and many of the distinctive elements in Israel's religion are closely associated with them. Their teaching was not generally acceptable in their own times, but much of it was preserved by a faithful few and thanks to them we have the prophecies to read and study. They expressed in the strongest possible terms their conviction that Israel is different from other peoples. Her leaders and rulers are different (2 Kings 3: 26, 27), her prophets are different from prophets in general (1 Kings 22: 10–18), her priests serve a cult which is different from other cults (2 Kings 11: 17, 18), some even of her social customs differ from those of her neighbours. Most of the time the prophets are condemning what is because it deviates from what should be and urging change to better ways.

See, I and the sons whom the LORD has given me
    are to be signs and portents in Israel,
sent by the LORD of Hosts who dwells on Mount Zion.
      But men will say to you,
'Seek guidance of ghosts and familiar spirits
    who squeak and gibber;
a nation may surely seek guidance of its gods,
of the dead on behalf of the living,
      for an oracle or a message?'
They will surely say some such thing as this;
      but what they say is futile. (Isa. 8: 18–20)

These were the words of the LORD to me: Prophesy, man, against the shepherds of Israel; prophesy and say to them, You shepherds, these are the words of the Lord GOD: How I hate the shepherds of Israel who care only for themselves! Should not the shepherd care for the sheep? You consume the milk, wear the wool, and slaughter the fat beasts, but you do not feed the sheep. You have not encouraged the weary, tended the sick, bandaged the hurt, recovered the straggler, or searched for the lost; and even the strong you have driven with ruthless severity. They are scattered, they have no shepherd, they have become the prey of wild beasts. My sheep go straying over the mountains and on every high hill, my flock is dispersed over the whole country, with no one to ask after them or search for them. (Ezek. 34: 1–6)

But the message was scarcely ever taken to heart.

Just as they did not listen to my words, says the LORD, when I took pains to send them my servants the prophets, so you did not listen, says the LORD. (Jer. 29: 19)

After David's time the frontiers of the kingdom were never again so well secured. After the division into two kingdoms there were times, under Omri for instance, when there was a considerable degree of prosperity and security. But the normal Palestine picture was of conflicts between the many kingdoms, of alliances made amongst them and of continual struggle to repel threats from Egypt in the south and from a succession of invaders from the north. The normal supposition among these kingdoms was that their individual gods were similarly involved in the power struggle: the gods of defeated nations were defeated gods, the gods of dominant nations were dominant gods. The Israelite prophets declared that Israel should stand aside from all these alliances and the conventions which governed the relations between their neighbours, large and small. Israel must be loyal to God even to the length of denying normal hospitality to gods of allies, for the claim was that God would defend and strengthen his own people if they depended on him alone. This was a theory that could never be put to the test and to the very end there were those who turned the argument the other way and complained that disaster had overtaken them because they had not faithfully observed the cult of the queen of heaven (Jer. 44: 15–19).

## (b) *Prophets and kings*

It was customary for kings to have not only military and political experts amongst their advisers, but also priests and prophets. It was not, however, usual for prophets to challenge and criticize the king's policies and decisions as Israel's prophets did. From Samuel (1 Sam. 13:6–14) and Nathan (2 Sam. 12:1–14) onwards there is a succession of men who interpreted public affairs and private behaviour in the light of their convictions about God's demands. These demands could well be different from the demands of the situation as judged by conventional standards, and frequently prophets clashed with kings. The prophetic claim is that God's authority is absolute, the king's is not. No king in Israel is free to behave as he chooses, even if other kings do (Amos 7:7–17).

Frequently prophets try to press home their message by describing the dire results of disobedience to the word of God. Their picture of the future is gloomy because their assessment of the present is poor. But their basic message is not about the future, gloomy or otherwise, it is about the present and the urgent necessity to be obedient to the commands of God who brought their forefathers from slavery in Egypt (Ezek. 33:10, 11).

## (c) *Prophets and priests*

Priests at the courts of kings and at other holy places were responsible for carrying out the requirements of the cult. A royal shrine was one of the complex of buildings associated with the king's palace which also included palaces for wives, quarters for guards, storehouses and so on (1 Kings 7). The leaders of Israel in the past had not been kings with city headquarters, they had moved from place to place and the shrine moved with them. On their journeys the Israelites had carried with them the Ark. In Joshua's time the Tent of the Presence in which it was housed was established at Shiloh (Josh. 18: 1), where the boy Samuel served under Eli and heard his call to prophesy (1 Sam. 2 and 3). After the war with the Philistines the Ark had no new permanent home until David brought it to Jerusalem, his new headquarters and capital city (2 Sam. 6). Wherever the Ark had been there had been a focal point for Israelite worship and this was now to be Jerusalem. Was the building of a temple to be a feature of the new settled life, suggesting that the Presence would be permanently there? or was Israel to be distinguished from her neighbours by having none, because God's Presence cannot be so confined?

It was Solomon who established an Israelite kingdom modelled on other kingdoms and built a royal shrine like other royal shrines. There is no evidence to suggest that prophets spoke against the building of a temple in Jerusalem at this time though later ones frequently condemned what was done in it. But there is a characteristically prophetic flavour in the account of the project:

> The word of the LORD came to Solomon, saying, 'As for this house which you are building, if you are obedient to my ordinances and conform to my precepts and loyally observe all my commands, then I will fulfil my promise to you, the promise I gave to your father David, and I will dwell among the Israelites and never forsake my people Israel.' (1 Kings 6:11–13)

When the northern tribes withdrew from the Jerusalem-based kingdom, Jeroboam set up shrines at Dan and

Bethel as focal points for his people (1 Kings 12: 25–33). Bethel was a royal shrine (Amos 7: 10–14) and Dan was probably the same. Later Omri built Samaria as a capital city and we are told that his son Ahab built a temple there – a temple to Baal (1 Kings 16: 31, 32). The prophet Elijah, however, strongly challenged king and people. 'How long will you sit on the fence? If the LORD is God, follow him; but if Baal, then follow him' (1 Kings 18: 21). Prophets in both kingdoms declare the same message: Israel, north and south alike, must worship only the Lord. Later generations of Israelite interpreters were descended from the Jerusalem-based part of Israel and they condemned all the worship in the northern kingdom because of what they called 'the sins into which Jeroboam son of Nebat had led Israel' (2 Kings 3: 3 and many other places). But even this heavy emphasis in the telling of the traditions of these times has not submerged the evidence that is in them of the more general prophetic concern – the concern that the Lord only should be worshipped, rather than a concern about particular places or persons or times.

The local places of worship, staffed by the local families of priests, were the focal points of the religion of the tribes even after they became constituent parts of a kingdom. These are referred to as the hill-shrines because they were sited on natural or artificially-made hills. Many of these were probably the shrines of the previous inhabitants and from the prophetic condemnation of many of them we must conclude that not only the place but its customs had been taken over. The prophets pleaded for reform, for a cult properly Israelite; they did not suggest that no worship at all should be offered in these places. The sad refrain of the later editors that even fairly 'good' kings did not sweep away the hill-shrines reflects a later point of view (1 Kings 15: 9–15). Until almost the end of the kingdom of Judah there were local shrines and local priests and local cults which may well have developed in different ways (Jer. 1: 1). Some of them may have been almost indistinguishable from what went before and others more in line with what the prophets pleaded for. Ways of worship were worked out along the same general lines but with different variations of detail, as we can now see in the books of Moses.

Two kings of Judah, Hezekiah and Josiah, are much commended in the tradition for 'reforming' religion by closing down the local hill-shrines and purging the Jerusalem temple of all traces of the worship of foreign gods and idols (2 Kings 18: 1–4; 23: 1–25). The story tells that the young king Josiah put the work in hand under the guidance of priests in Jerusalem; these were presumably priests who had not been able to influence the policies of king Manasseh. The proposal that all holy places except the Jerusalem temple should be eliminated could have been made because those priests believed, rightly or wrongly, that the cult there was beyond reform. Or it could have been because they believed that there should be only one place for sacrifice and that was Jerusalem. On the other hand it might well have been pointed out that every possible offence had been committed in Jerusalem and that the priests there were guilty beyond recovery whereas some other places might have had a simpler, purer cult.

From their earliest days Israel and Judah have been doing what is wrong in my eyes, provoking me to anger by their actions, says the LORD. For this city has so roused my anger and my fury, from the time it was built down to this day, that I would rid myself of it. Israel and Judah, their kings, officers, priests, prophets, and everyone living in Jerusalem and Judah have provoked me to anger by their wrongdoing. They have turned their backs on me and averted their faces; though I took pains to teach them, they would not hear or learn their lesson. They set up their loathsome idols in the house which bears my name and so defiled it. They built shrines to Baal in the Valley of Ben-hinnom, to surrender their sons and daughters to Molech. It was no command of mine, nor did it ever enter my thought to do this abominable thing and lead Judah into sin. (Jer. 32: 30-5)

The conflicts here are not between the loyal and the disloyal but between different understandings of what loyalty involves. In fact the Jerusalem party won the day and most of the traditions come down to us from them through their successors. But this does not mean that we have to accept their crushing condemnation of everyone else. They interpreted the political fall of Israel as punishment for the sins of Israel. But others who believed this just as strongly identified the sins differently: some thought there should never have been kings, some that no temple should have been built anywhere, some even that Israelites should never have settled down to living in houses and towns at all.

## (d) *Prophets after the kingdoms*

When the Assyrians guarded against any possible resistance by interchanging populations, the resulting mixed peoples carried on the kind of worship they were used to, closely related to the land where they were living (2 Kings 17: 24-33). When the Babylonians transported all who they thought might cause any trouble, the priests who remained in and around Jerusalem carried on somehow or other. Those who were deported took traditions with them, some perhaps written down (including some collections of what prophets had said) but much stored in the memory.

The Babylonians were sufficiently sure of themselves not to treat their captives harshly. They had taken out of conquered countries enough of the civil, military and religious leaders to make sure that no revolt could be organized; Babylonian officials administered the other- wise helpless people in the conquered territories. So those who had been deported were free enough to be able to observe what went on around them and free to organize themselves to preserve as far as possible their own way of life. Priests, whose work had been so closely associated with the temple, could not carry out their sacrificial functions; but they still had their responsibility for teaching and could make preparations for the day when they or their successors would once again perform the sacrifices in Jerusalem. Prophets, called to interpret any and every situation, found plenty of work to do. In their new environment many things were on a larger scale than anything they had been accustomed to in Jerusalem and in particular they must have been most forcibly struck by the magnificence of the Babylonian gods. These huge monsters were carried in procession on festival occasions and thoughtful Israelites must have seen them with astonishment and even incredulity. Prophets found them a great occasion for exposing the absurdity of all idol-worship. The bigger the images, the more obvious that they are the work of men's hands, the more ludicrous that men should put their trust in them (Isa. 44: 12–20).

Size may bring home dramatically the futility and offence of idolatry, but even the smallest of images is equally deplorable. Many religious images were originally signs to mark places where gods might visit or reminders of their presence and their power. But almost always they came to be seen as representations, and for the prophets who spoke to Israel in exile the golden calves at Bethel and Dan which fellow-Israelites had revered in the past and all the strange gods which had been entertained in Jerusalem from time to time were, and always had been, abominations. They had always been wrong because they were foreign in Israel but they are utterly offensive and futile in themselves because they are of man's making.

God is the maker of man, which is why the worship of idols is just nonsense. It is just as much nonsense in Babylon as in Israel, for God is maker of Babylonians as well as Israelites, and he is everywhere present and everywhere to be worshipped. Not only is it absurd to worship idols, it is equally absurd to suppose that there are many gods, even for every nation to worship its own god or gods. If man's worship is to have any meaning for him, any dignity and purpose, he can only worship one invisible God. Prophets of the time of the exile claim that they and their ancestors have always believed in and worshipped this true God. During this time the old traditions were newly illumined by the new insights and re-interpreted in the light of them. Even old traditions which can only with difficulty be transformed in this way, and yet were too venerable to be discarded, took on new authority because they were brought into association with the patriarchs.

Listen to me, all who follow the right and seek the LORD:
   look to the rock from which you were hewn,
     to the quarry from which you were dug;

look to your father Abraham
   and to Sarah who gave you birth:
when I called him he was but one,
   I blessed him and made him many. (Isa. 51: 1, 2)

And now the LORD who formed me in the womb to be
     his servant,
   to bring Jacob back to him
   that Israel should be gathered to him,
   now the LORD calls me again:
   it is too slight a task for you, as my servant,
   to restore the tribes of Jacob,
     to bring back the descendants of Israel:
   I will make you a light to the nations,
   to be my salvation to earth's farthest bounds.
                        (Isa. 49: 5, 6)

Abraham, Jacob and many others are seen now in the
Old Testament in this great light of belief in one God who
rules universally and who caused the world to exist from
its beginning.

This was the belief of a small number of the remains of
a thoroughly defeated small nation. They looked to a
future time when Israel would be re-established in
Jerusalem, when God would be worthily worshipped in
the temple there and the whole world would recognize
his supremacy and their leadership. But meanwhile Israel
herself must be gathered together again, must learn her
vocation and learn to obey God's law. Many in exile
devoted themselves to preparation for this by working
over the law that they had and making sure that it would
be preserved for future use, as well as observed by themselves so far as it could be in a foreign land. The numerous
traditions and codes which they had brought with them,
some in writing, some in their memories, were worked on

and organized so as to be a basis for the future. The basis
of their belief in themselves lay in their confidence that
they were the true descendants of those to whom God
had revealed his will and his plan and who had been
obedient to the calling. God's purpose for them had been
most clearly shown in his bringing them from Egypt to
Canaan and now they expected a second deliverance, to
bring them from another captivity back to Jerusalem.
Last time there had been much to learn, this time they
would be armed with knowledge about what they ought
to do and how to do it.

Listen to the word of the LORD, you nations,
announce it, make it known to coasts and islands far away:
   He who scattered Israel shall gather them again
and watch over them as a shepherd watches his flock.
For the LORD has ransomed Jacob
and redeemed him from a foe too strong for him.
They shall come with shouts of joy to Zion's height,
shining with happiness at the bounty of the LORD,
the corn, the new wine, and the oil,
   the young of flock and herd. (Jer. 31: 10–12)

After the oracles and poems which witness to the
expectation of a triumphant return to Jerusalem there are
some which relate to the time after parties had gone to
Jerusalem and were struggling in conditions very different
from the earlier hopes (Hag. 1: 1–11). When Israelite
worship and the Israelite way of life were established in
Jerusalem in line with Persian policy, the fervour of prophetic interpretation developed new forms of expression.
A new context posed new questions and required new
methods of confrontation and the new prophetic approach
can be traced elsewhere in the Old Testament as, for
example, in the sermon forms used in Chronicles.

## The book of Psalms

Some of the psalms, or songs, may be later than the latest oracles in the Prophets; but there are also many very old poems included here and some which would have been familiar for many generations. Over and over again comment had been added, and with time the additions came to be part of an ever-growing poem. Whatever their various origins, probably at different holy places, these poems became closely associated with the later temple and in them are to be found declarations of Israel's beliefs expressed in a most dramatic form.

There are poems here about the wonders of creation and God's control over it (e.g. Ps. 104). There are numerous references to the crossing of the sea and God's activity in saving Israel from the pursuing Pharaoh (e.g. Ps. 105). There are psalms which emphasize the severity of God (e.g. Ps. 11) and others which speak more of his love and his mercy (e.g. Ps. 32). There are some which speak of him in ancient homely terms (e.g. Ps. 18: 1–6) and others which dwell on his majesty and power (e.g. Ps. 67). Very many of the psalms were used at the times of the great festivals when the great happenings of the past were recalled. Israel offered thanks and praise to God for his greatness and his goodness (e.g. Ps. 111). Circumstances were often much less favourable, both for the community and for the individual, and many psalms lament the misfortunes that have overtaken Israel (e.g. Ps. 40). Many express repentance for sin and ask that God will take away the guilt of his people (e.g. Ps. 130). Here in particular psalms are often expressing what prophets too have expressed and in similar form (Mic. 7).

If we read psalms and think of them as having been

known and heard by the people who came for the offering of sacrifice in their villages or towns or at the temple in Jerusalem we shall have some idea of what the religion had come to be. Psalm 66 shows how the praise of God is associated with the offering of sacrifice in the temple and Psalm 51 expresses in profound terms the awareness that man must put away his sin before he can hope that his sacrifices will be acceptable to God. Psalm 119 is a great declaration of devotion to God and his law, expressed in very personal terms. The time came when yet another lesson had to be learned, the lesson that every individual Israelite is called to individual personal loyalty and obedience. Time had been when it seemed that individual leaders were all-important; later the people as a whole had had a part to play and now to these is added the inescapable responsibility to be carried by every individual.

The time is coming, says the LORD, when I will make a new covenant with Israel and Judah. It will not be like the covenant I made with their forefathers when I took them by the hand and led them out of Egypt. Although they broke my covenant, I was patient with them, says the LORD. But this is the covenant which I will make with Israel after those days, says the LORD; I will set my law within them and write it on their hearts; I will become their God and they shall become my people. No longer need they teach one another to know the LORD; all of them, high and low alike, shall know me, says the LORD, for I will forgive their wrongdoing and remember their sin no more. (Jer. 31: 31-4)

## The legacy of prophecy

This religion 'of Israel' is the religion that has grown up within Israel, not the religion of the people as a whole. The great prophets who were its great pioneers had disciples who remembered and passed on the teaching of their masters. Most of this teaching is found in the books of Prophets. By the time these ideas had taken shape and had begun to have some influence the descendants of the first settlers were dispersed widely and many of them had intermarried with neighbouring tribes and were indistinguishable from them. There were identifiable groups of Israelites who married only among themselves in many places outside Palestine, but little is known about the religion of these groups at this early date. The evidence provided by the oracles of the prophets shows that even in the home country the old ideas were more powerful than the new ones. As for the situation in the other parts of the world, it would have been extremely unlikely that any of the peoples of the growing empires would have taken any notice of the claims of a group of subject foreigners, even if they knew anything about them.

Yet by the time of the publication of the New English Bible, some twenty-five centuries since the beginning of the resettlement in Jerusalem, this religion and two others closely related to it have spread all over the world and now have millions of adherents. The books of what are now called by Christians 'Old Testament' and 'Apocrypha' have been studied, cherished, translated and venerated continuously. The millions are still far from being the total of the world's population but they do show that these basic ideas have survived and have commended themselves to many.

But the new ideas about the uniqueness of God and the status of man and the special responsibilities of the people charged with making this known to the world at large were at first understood and accepted by only a very few. Amongst these few, different expectations for the future began to develop and different ways of reacting to political circumstances. The hope of re-establishment in Jerusalem was fulfilled, though scarcely in triumph, and the next chapter began. Even when it was possible for some to make a new beginning in Jerusalem only a few took advantage of the opportunity. This does not mean that those who remained in other countries were not loyal to the traditions of their forefathers: they were known and distinguished by their special way of life and their devotion to it. Those who went to Jerusalem and who organized life there and restored the temple were those for whom Jerusalem was an essential focal point for the life of God's people in the world.

The opening passage of the first group of Old Testament books witnesses to the belief in the power of God's word in creation. The opening passage of the book of Psalms expresses devotion to God's word as it has been revealed to man. The study of this revelation, its interpretation and its application to new circumstances, is the main task for later generations. What has been inherited is open to varying interpretations and so gives rise to different parties and to conflicts between them. There was disagreement about one point in particular which had been taken for granted for a very long time. It was generally supposed, indeed it frequently still is, that if people were to behave properly they would prosper. Conversely it can be taken for granted that failure and disaster must be the result of error.

The LORD knows each day of the good man's life,
and his inheritance shall last for ever.
   When times are bad, he shall not be distressed,
and in days of famine he shall have enough.
   But the wicked shall perish,
and their children shall beg their bread. (Ps. 37: 18–20)

Much energy can be devoted to identifying the error, to retrieving it and ensuring against any repetition. But if the explanations offered are so unsatisfactory that the basic proposition is challenged then another revolution threatens. For if the simple cause-and-effect explanation fails there is either no explanation or there must be a different kind of explanation altogether. Even if the cause-and-effect is the sin-and-punishment sequence the explanation may not be a simple one because it may not be easy to decide what the sin was. The revolution happened because serious-minded people could not be convinced any longer. Equally serious-minded people defended the old position and worked hard at their explanations.

It was the pressure of external as well as internal conflicts which forced the next developments. The traditions of Law and Prophets were well established and continued to be a main guide as they have been for centuries. But there were other books and others yet to be written. Some of these are also in the Old Testament and came to have comparable authority by the time that the second Jerusalem period ended, once again in disaster. This disaster was even worse than anything that had happened to them before because all Jews, as they were called by then, were expelled from the city and none were allowed to enter the new city which was built in its place.

## THE MOST RECENT PAST OF THE ISRAELITES – THE OTHER BOOKS IN THE OLD TESTAMENT AND THE APOCRYPHA

### Religion in Israel under Persian rule

Assyrians aimed at destroying the individuality of the peoples they conquered by breaking them up and mixing them so as to make sure there was no revolt: so far as we know this policy was successful against the tribes whose capital city had been Samaria. Babylonians deported any who might stir people to revolt and appointed governors to ensure the preservation of law and order. This is the policy which preserved intact the various élites of the kingdom whose capital city had been Jerusalem. When the Persians overthrew Babylonian power they inherited the results of this policy and their own was to send parties back to their countries of origin to re-establish their own way of life there. We know that from 538 B.C. onwards a succession of expeditions went to Jerusalem, that the city was restored and worship organized in the temple. There were similar developments in Samaria but we hear less about them.

### Worship in Jerusalem

The city of Jerusalem and its temple precinct must have been in a sorry state. Instead of the great structure which had been the ideal, fitted out with everything necessary for performing an elaborate ritual, only the ruins of the old remained; the altar itself was broken down. Instead of a long-established faithful priesthood staffing the complex of buildings in undisputed authority, there were the last remains of a company who, according to many, were the descendants of those who had been a main cause of past disasters. But the newcomers brought with them detailed traditions about what should be done and boasted the authority of Moses. This paramount authority had now been transmitted to those who, according to this same tradition, were members of a true priesthood.

In the books of Ezra and Nehemiah stories are told of expeditions coming from Babylon with authority from Cyrus to build a temple in Jerusalem, of Nehemiah's work of rebuilding the city, of conflict with the people of Samaria, of various attempts to bring life in Jerusalem up to the standards required by the idealists. These two books must have been produced in their present form some time after the events of which they tell, otherwise it is not likely that Artaxerxes I and Artaxerxes II would have been confused with each other, as it seems they have been. The two books of Chronicles together with Ezra and Nehemiah give us, however, a very clear picture of what the editor, and the people for whom he speaks, judged to be of prime importance.

It was their unshakable conviction that Jerusalem is first and foremost the setting for the worship of God. For them the great kings of the past were David who made the preparations and Solomon who carried out his plans and built the temple on the site purchased by David for the purpose (1 Chron. 21: 18–22: 1). Such men came to Jerusalem with the primary object of establishing worship there in what they had come to believe to be the way that God requires. The elaborate furnishings and fittings and rituals which they planned were not centred on any tremendous representation of a deity, not on anything visible at all. The holiest place of all would be an empty place, witnessing to the mystery of God who is everywhere present, but who from time to time may express his particular presence in Jerusalem amongst his people. This temple was the successor to the Tent of the Presence which the journeying Israelites carried with them and which is described with such a wealth of imaginative detail in the traditions of the far past (Exod. 35-40). In those old stories God's presence was indicated by the coming of a cloud (40: 34); in the same tradition God's acceptance of Solomon's building was shown by the coming of a cloud (2 Chron. 5: 13). Ezekiel's vision of a future temple (Ezek. 40: 1 – 44: 3) includes the same sign of his presence (43: 5). The empty holy place is a continual reminder that God cannot be conjured up at man's will. He is always and everywhere present but may from time to time express his presence by special signs. The temple is planned as a continual reminder that man must wait upon God, must present himself before God as an expression of his dependence upon God and at the same time of the power and majesty of God.

The vehicle of the new beliefs in the restored temple was the old sacrificial round, still similar to what had been the general pattern. The round of the year, of the week, of the day, are reminders of the belief that God creates, that he redeems, that he requires man's response in recognition and obedience. The recognition is expressed by the very existence of the temple and by the carrying out of the prescribed round of ceremonies by the prescribed officials, the true priests. The priests have inherited this responsibility and it includes teaching the people about the part they have to play and the significance of what they, the priests, are doing on their behalf. The restoration was understood as an expression of God's will – his will to forgive past failure. In response to this the rituals of purification were interpreted to express Israel's sense of failure and need for forgiveness.

It is only too obvious that any round of ceremonies can become mechanical and meaningless if the purpose of the ritual is obscured. Nevertheless those parts of the Old Testament which are particularly concerned with cere-monial worship are inspired by the belief that these forms of worship have been decreed by the invisible universal God. This implies that God can truly be worshipped by means that man has learnt to use, however inadequate these might otherwise seem to be. Man must use the methods he has inherited from the past when he has transformed them to express more profound beliefs. This spirit is expressed frequently and with a wealth of poetry and imagination in the book of Psalms.

> Acclaim the LORD, all men on earth,
>   worship the LORD in gladness;
> enter his presence with songs of exultation.
> Know that the LORD is God;
> he has made us and we are his own,
>   his people, the flock which he shepherds.
> Enter his gates with thanksgiving
>   and his courts with praise.
> Give thanks to him and bless his name;
> for the LORD is good and his love is everlasting,
>   his constancy endures to all generations. (Ps. 100)

## Worship in other places

Within the main body of the tradition it has been accepted that only in Jerusalem can sacrificial worship be carried out. It is the archaeologists who have told us that there was a group of Jews in Egypt who had a temple of their own in their settlement (see p. 88). We know too that groups of faithful Israelites, living in various countries where their fathers had been forcibly settled, could and did meet together to recall solemnly in mind and heart the temple and all it stood for. They could send money for its support and beautification and they could hope from time to time to visit it. They had the Law, in which the feasts were described and their significance spelled out; this they could study under the guidance of those of their number who had become learned in these matters. When they met together to mark their own particular observances and to reinforce the bonds that held them together they would read and expound the scriptures. These Israelites living in foreign parts became devoted to the word of God as it has been gathered in written form and to those outside they began to look like a people devoted to a book.

## Social organization

There is more in the book than tradition and instructions about worship; there are instructions about almost every aspect of social and family life. Before Israel could stand as witness to the world these too had to be carried out; and they presented some major problems. Who were to be counted as Israelites to be trained and supported to give this witness? How was the training to be organized and what form should it take? If Israel included all the scattered peoples how were they to be gathered in?

It was possible to set about organizing affairs in Jerusalem according to the Law as it then stood and this work was taken in hand. One past 'error' had been inter-marriage with non-Israelites: this was forbidden and must cease. The sabbath, too, must be properly observed (e.g. Neh. 13). No aspect of living is outside the concern and control of God's word and command. God is over all and this is why man can only be truly himself when his living conforms to this understanding.

> Thou didst descend upon Mount Sinai and speak with them from heaven, and give them right judgements and true laws, and statutes and commandments which were good, and thou didst make known to them thy holy sabbath and give them commandments, statutes, and laws through thy servant Moses. (Neh. 9: 13, 14)

When Israel shows to the world this kind of living the world will recognize it as the true life for man, will want to follow the same way and will recognize the God whose way it is.

Meanwhile there were more short-term objectives. Israel had to survive if anything was to be achieved at all, but this could easily become an end in itself and when it did it aroused protest from some who saw it as a betrayal. The determination to survive as a distinct people led to a very tight definition of membership. The only kind of definition which could be applied practically covered many for whom religion and the Law were not of primary importance and excluded others whose concerns were more truly those of devotion to God and to a thoughtful understanding of his demands. So protest grew against strict application of the test of pedigree as illustrated in the story of Ruth and greater emphasis was laid on motives and general principles. This kind of challenge to the official position was not a questioning of the underlying matters of faith in the one God and his purposes for Israel; but doubts were expressed about some of the deductions made from them. Because all parties were seriously involved and determined that Israel should be her true self the controversy was lasting and sometimes bitter; it was never resolved.

While the Persians retained control the Israelites made full use of the opportunity to establish their own way of life in Jerusalem and the country round. This was not a uniform pattern of social and religious customs, though some worked hard to make it so. It was a way of life based upon beliefs about human life which held different implications for different groups of people and which made religion a living issue among them. In this they seem to have been unusual, because most of the old religions of the past had not developed and so they had lost all significance for people and had fallen into decay. By the time the comparatively peaceful Persian period came to an end Israel's religion had grown to be a vital focus of Israelite loyalty.

Arguments about what ought to be done, what decisions should be taken, what choices are open, are always carried on against the background of what actually happens. Just as in all societies religions have developed and with them priests and prophets, so in all societies there have been those who have skilfully and memorably described human beings in terms of how they carry on their relationships with one another. As there are many common human characteristics so there are many common proverbs, brief statements of fact not in the first place implying any moral judgement but simply describing common experience.

> An anxious heart dispirits a man,
> and a kind word fills him with joy. (Prov. 12: 25)

The man whose observations and descriptions commend themselves as true to general experience is a wise man and commands respect and confidence; his guidance and advice are likely to be sound and practical. In many societies proverbial sayings of this kind accumulated and were collected and written down and known as 'Sayings of the Wise'. Because in many respects people behave in the same ways in different societies it is not surprising that the same observations were made and many similar proverbial sayings are found in different places. (See *The Making of the Old Testament*, pp. 40–4.)

In Israel too there were wise men and there were proverbs, many the same as those of neighbours, but because these sayings are not expressed as moral exhortations, and the ruling concern of the powerful prophetic movement was moral, they have not grown into the great accumulation of Mosaic Law. Wisdom was nevertheless highly regarded, and one group of traditions about Solomon acclaims him for his wisdom, meaning his powers of accurate observation both of nature and of human nature (1 Kings 4: 29–34; 3: 16–28). As time went on, however, shrewd observation and the conclusions drawn from it were inevitably drawn into the orbit of the debate about God and his ways with man.

## *Wisdom*

Simple, clear description of the results of what we do can be the equivalent of advice, even of encouragement to behave in one way rather than another; gradually proverbial sayings can come to have the force of moral sayings even if they are not directly associated with commands.

> Better be slow to anger than a fighter,
> better govern one's temper than capture a city.
>
> (Prov. 16: 32)

Observation can also lead to statements which directly, or by implication, challenge judgements which are generally accepted or which are strongly canvassed, as, for instance, that good conduct always pays:

> In my empty existence I have seen it all, from a righteous man perishing in his righteousness to a wicked man growing old in his wickedness. (Eccles. 7: 15)

This kind of statement, which may seem to many to be somewhat cynical, is, after all, true to common observation. A real debate develops because of the difference between what can be expected on the basis of a simple theory of rewards and punishments and what honest observation must report. On the one hand the discrepancy is explained by defending the assumption and then going on to say that what was thought to be good was actually mistaken. This view leads to greater and greater efforts to ensure that good is really done by breaking the requirements down into such small units that it is in the end impossible to make a mistake. The weaknesses and superficiality of this approach are obvious. Another approach to the problem is to challenge the assumption itself:

> When things go well, be glad; but when things go ill, consider this: God has set the one alongside the other in such a way that no one can find out what is to happen next. (Eccles. 7: 14)

There is yet another way, perhaps rather a frightening way, certainly not a way followed easily. This is to question God's ways of administering the laws that only he can have made. After going over the ground again and again from every possible point of view the debate presented in the book of Job is unresolved.

I would plead the whole record of my life
and present that in court as my defence. (Job 31: 37)

Man's dilemma remains. God's ways after all are past
finding out, but this does not mean that man can be truly
man unless he pursues the way of understanding and
obedience. He can be sure of God, he cannot be equally
sure of himself. He depends on God for all that he is and
has, including his understanding with its limitations.

But the Almighty we cannot find; his power is beyond
    our ken,
and his righteousness not slow to do justice.
Therefore mortal men pay him reverence,
and all who are wise look to him. (Job 37: 23, 24)

### New developments under Greek rule

The Persians dominated much of Asia for nearly 200 years
and Israel, though not independent, was free to develop
her own characteristic religious culture. But Persian
power was threatened from the west and after fierce
confrontations on the frontier between Asia and Europe
the Greeks broke through. In 334 B.C. Alexander marched
to the eastern border of the Persian territory. For the next
200 years and more the rulers of the whole vast area were
Greek. The Greeks themselves were divided and torn by
war after Alexander's death but they retained control over
the territories he had conquered.

The Greek kings who ruled in Palestine were not themselves philosophers, but their policies reflected the way
that Greek societies had developed. In all the lands which
they overran, cities were built on a large scale, better
planned and in larger numbers than had been known
before. This was a work of benefit and improvement for

they took it as without question that urban life is better and fuller than the unsophisticated country pattern. In these cities were gathered the many elements which by that time were to be found all over the area. But the organization and the amenities were like those of Greek towns elsewhere: games and the theatre were part of the pattern of life and most people appreciated them. These were an education for the population in general: the encouragement of bodily health and strength by exercise and the dramatic presentation of the issues of life and death on the stage.

Action and colour enlivened existence and no one had any objection to all this except those who, because they could find no sanction for such things in the Mosaic Law, condemned them outright. This widened the gap between some Jewish leaders and the ordinary people. The leaders themselves were divided; for some were totally opposed to Greek ways, while others recognized that they expressed a confidence in human living which was in harmony with their own understanding of man as having a special place and responsibility in God's work.

Alexander lived only ten years after his swift conquests, but during that time he had set on foot the characteristic urbanization policy and as a result of it the many peoples and cultures in that widespread area were brought face to face. These confrontations were on the whole fruitful, though clashes and conflicts would get more notice, just as they would today. This mixing fell short of the Greek objective of imposing Greek ways entirely. To the Greeks their own way of life and their own language were so manifestly superior to any other that they were slow to appreciate that others might be equally attached to their inherited traditions and beliefs. Greeks were prepared to be all-embracing and did not understand that this was not universally attractive, still less that at least one religion was very much alive and very exclusive. These strange phenomena did not as yet constitute any political threat and the Greek kings were so much occupied with their own efforts to establish their frontiers that they saw no danger signals here at first.

To the north in Asia and to the south in Egypt the situation locally was more peaceful than in Palestine. It was in such places that there developed the new strand of Judaism, taking to itself ways of interpreting the universe in contemplation and poetry which harmonized so well with Jewish meditation on the creator God and his law. All Jewish communities had emotional and historical loyalty to Jerusalem and the Mosaic Law, but outside Jerusalem these loyalties had to be observed in new ways, even in another language.

A legacy of great value has come to us through the law, the prophets, and the writers who followed in their steps, and for this Israel's traditions of discipline and wisdom deserve recognition. It is the duty of those who study the scriptures not only to become expert themselves, but also to use their scholarship for the benefit of the outside world through both the spoken and the written word. So my grandfather Jesus, who had applied himself industriously to the study of the law, the prophets, and the other writings of our ancestors, and had gained a considerable proficiency in them, was moved to compile a book of his own on the themes of discipline and wisdom, so that, with this further help, scholars might make greater progress in their studies by living as the law directs.

You are asked then to read with sympathetic attention, and make allowances if, in spite of all the devoted work I have put into the translation, some of the expressions appear inadequate. For it is impossible for a translator to find precise equivalents for the original Hebrew in another language. Not only with this book, but with the law, the prophets, and the rest of the writings, it makes no small difference to read them in the original.

When I came to Egypt and settled there in the thirty-eighth year of the reign of King Euergetes, I found great scope for education; and I thought it very necessary to spend some energy and labour on the translation of this book. Ever since then I have been applying my skill night and day to complete it, and to publish it for the use of those who have made their home in a foreign land, and wish to become scholars by training themselves to live according to the law. (Ecclus. Preface)

To transpose the religion of Yahweh into another language and strange thought-forms would at one time have seemed impossible and even when it was actually being done some had reservations about it. But Greek, with its different vocabulary and its rich literature, provided a yet wider field to explore in the pursuit of the impossible, the expression in language of man's insights into the nature of things.

I thought this over in my mind, and I perceived that in kinship with wisdom lies immortality and in her friendship is pure delight; that in doing her work is wealth that cannot fail, to be taught in her school gives understanding, and an honourable name is won by converse with her. So I went about in search of some way to win her for my own. As a child I was born to excellence, and a noble soul fell to my lot; or rather, I myself was noble, and I entered into an unblemished body; but I saw that there was no way to gain possession of her except by gift of God – and it was a mark of understanding to know from whom that gift must come. (Wisd. of Sol. 8: 17–21)

Although Jews in Palestine had special problems to contend with, and particular concerns for Jerusalem, the beliefs which all held in common were the most powerful factor in the relationships between Jews all over the world. The belief that God whom they worshipped is the only true God carried with it the conviction that this must eventually be the universal belief. So they all looked to a time when Israel would be supreme in the world. They envisaged this in many different ways but all had some form of expectation. This was the strongest possible incentive for keeping their traditions and their way of life alive, continually looking forward to the fulfilment of the vocation of God's people.

> For, as the new heavens and the new earth
> which I am making shall endure in my sight,
>     says the LORD,
> so shall your race and your name endure;
>     and month by month at the new moon,
>         week by week on the sabbath,
> all mankind shall come to bow down before me,
>     says the LORD. (Isa. 66: 22, 23)

### Political hopes

Over and over again in the past there had been the hope that the collapse of an empire might mean intervention to bring Israel to power. When Assyria, Babylon, Persia declined, Israel's hope of triumph flourished, but it had never yet been fulfilled. Many of the leaders of priestly groups associated with the temple were willing to accept Greek ways and for the time being at any rate to submit to Greek rule. In opposition to them was a patriotic nationalist group who regarded this as disloyal appeasement. When Antiochus IV departed from the policy of his predecessors and tried to insist that Jews should conform to foreign religious practices there was revolt. After the success of the revolt the leaders made a bid for independence and their bid was successful: the books of Maccabees give us versions of these events. The Hasmonaean kings were not by any means what many Jews looked for as the rulers of a restored Davidic kingdom and although they had considerable political success they failed to establish a united Israel.

The conflicts among the Jews, among the Greeks, between Greeks and Jews, were at their height when the Romans arrived in the area – yet one more foreign rule to be endured. But Judaism survived as a way of life, definable in terms of its own beliefs, vindicating the efforts of all those of earlier generations who had worked and suffered to secure this very result. Judaism was well established in most of the territories which the Romans took over in forms whose very variety shows the strength of what all held in common. Even the conflicts within the Judaism of Palestine highlighted the vitality of their positions.

After the fall of Jerusalem in A.D. 70 many faithful Jews were left in Palestine to maintain the life of the nation as best they could, trying to make sure that nothing else was lost. They had the Law, the Prophets, the Psalms and other books. The Law, with its expectation of settlement in Canaan, and the Prophets, with the expectation of return to Palestine, stood clearly and now with very great authority as the witness to Israel's call and hope. But by now this religion had grown into a more complex and varied pattern of beliefs. The recent centuries of violence and controversy are themselves part of the story of Israel's religion because some of the conflicts were caused by religious differences and also because many different circumstances encouraged the development of many different aspects of this same religion. Not only did Israel survive, she survived in strength because of wide diversity springing from basic unity.

Jews abroad already had books in addition to the Law and the Prophets which they judged to be true to the tradition, even though some of them had been quite recently written and even written in Greek. It seems that they also had some of the same books as were in use in Palestine but in different versions or editions; the books of Daniel and Esther are examples. Baruch, too, and the Letter of Jeremiah have obvious links with the book of Jeremiah. These are amongst the books now known as 'Apocrypha', which has come to stand for 'books included in the Greek Bible but not included in the Hebrew Bible'.

*Hero stories*

Ruth, Esther, Tobit and Judith are all stories of individual determination and heroism in the face of challenges to Israel's way of life and beliefs. Daniel, too, is a story of resistance in Babylon, probably published at the time of the Maccabaean revolt to encourage all the faithful to refuse to eat foreign foods and make foreign sacrifices. The books of Maccabees themselves are material for what might have grown into yet another venerable tradition about loyalty to Yahweh and to Jerusalem but the Maccabaean heroes were only of recent times and even in their heyday some parties in Judaism had been critical of them, of their policies and their methods. More recently still a similar outbreak of violent revolt had been largely responsible for the worst of disasters.

## Apocalyptic

Chapters 7 to 12 of the book of Daniel are called 'Daniel's visions'. They are an example of apocalyptic writing in which the claim is that the hero, or holy man, has seen 'behind the veil' (*apocalypse* means 'unveiling'). These are revelations of what God plans to do, not unlike Ezekiel's great visions of a new Jerusalem, yet mostly of a somewhat violent sort, furnished with strange beasts and often set in an unnatural world. There are apocalyptic visions in 2 Esdras and in other books which have been preserved, though not in either the Hebrew or the Greek Bibles. (See *The Making of the Old Testament*, pp. 77–82.) Most of them promise violent revenge upon the heathen, widespread destruction of the world because it is evil and the establishment of Israel, or at any rate a remnant, to rebuild on the wreckage, or in a 'new' world. God appears as having been driven to desperation by the human race to the point of destroying most of it. This conflicts with the traditional form of the story of the flood where the rainbow appears as the sign of God's promise never again to destroy the earth (Gen. 9: 8–17).

Such horrifying 'hopes' (e.g. 2 Esdras 15) are desperate and seem to many to be signs of a failure of faith. They flourish in situations where expectations have not been fulfilled. Instead of taking a cool, second look at the expectations these writers have transposed their fulfilment into another world, arbitrarily imposed on top of our familiar one. Such a transposition can be interpreted as a surrender to the problem of evil, to the mistake of thinking that this is a problem which man has to solve by himself here. If man fails, as he has done, then the struggle can only be carried on elsewhere where God in person will take a hand. The transposition can also be seen as a logical and courageous development of the belief in God as creator and saviour. If God had taken a direct hand in creation, as Jews believed he had, and also at the moment of escape from slavery in Egypt – why not again? This form of hope and expectation adds another item to the accumulation of evidence for the unshakable belief of Israelites in the infinite power of God.

## Judaism in the world at large

The Jewish War must have been deeply distressing for Jews outside Palestine, though its practical impact was less devastating for them than for those whose land was laid waste. This dramatic moment brings to an end the story of the gathering of the Old Testament books, though not the story of the religion to which they witness – this is still going on. The story of the books covered some centuries, but not nearly such a long stretch of time as the story of the religion itself.

The oldest of the old traditions stopped growing at different times so that in some of them God can appear as though he were a character in the story, powerful and mysterious but at times almost embarrassingly human. Sometimes he is more like an erratic magician, almost less than human, and certainly not to be relied upon. These traditions survived because they were about the first beginnings of the people Israel, so important to their successors. In a less crude form the belief that God is active in history survived and developed to become one of the characteristics of Israel's religion. The critical sphere of God's activity is this world and the human community which inhabits it. God has made the heavens and he rules sun, moon and stars, but his deepest concern is with the affairs of men. He strives for the establishment of his rule over man, not by force but through man's free recognition of God as ultimately powerful and wise. If this were recognized, the affairs of men would be controlled by laws which are the true laws for man. God has been leading man towards the discovery of these laws particularly through his own people Israel to whom they have been revealed.

The great emphasis in some parts of the Old Testament on the terrible consequences of Israel's disobedience leaves a somewhat sombre impression. These oracles of doom and destruction were preserved and quoted by those who believed that there must be such a direct relation between religious practice and political future. These same people were urgently concerned to prevent the same things happening again because of their belief that the true destiny of man is not disaster and destruction but peace and prosperity. If man is to fulfil this destiny he has to learn to live according to his true nature and part of that nature is his ability to understand and participate. This is the conviction most startlingly expressed, at the beginning of Genesis, in the description of man as made in God's image (Gen. 1: 26, 27).

Israelites had also learned to adopt and recast ideas which had originated elsewhere. The process had been going on for centuries but we have books which are the product of the well-developed process. This process had not been the common one of syncretism – a word of Greek origin for the kind of uneasy mixture of religions which the prophets inveighed against during the period of the kingdoms. It is the adoption of words and ideas which, though different in form, are harmonious in substance with Jewish belief. The crucial point of contact was the confidence that man is endowed with powers which give him the opportunity to live within his environment and yet have a degree of control over it. This is a 'high' doctrine of man. The Jews had this doctrine along with a 'high' doctrine of God, whereas the old gods and goddesses of the Greeks no longer commanded even respect, certainly not reverence. The great qualities of human life, power, wisdom, love, rectitude, had for the Greeks become objectives in themselves. For the Jew all these qualities were both the creation and the character of God, the supreme power.

These doctrines of God and man assert the inestimable value of this world and man's life within it. They have grown out of experience in the past and thoughtful interpretation of that experience. They encourage the hope of a near present which will fulfil God's purposes undistorted by man's reluctance and sin. Speculations about a more distant future have scarcely yet begun, any more than questions about the nature and story of God before the making of the universe which man can observe. Most of the judgements and the hopes are still centred on Israel and the call to her to become fit to be the witness to the rest of mankind. But the whole human race is involved, it is mankind that is made in God's image and all are called to the great experience of knowing that they are created and loved by him.

To project hopes for the future on to a different plane is to open up the idea that there may be life for man other than the normal span of his living on this earth. If man's life is not bounded by individual birth and death, if his experience is to be not only the experience of the physical world we know, many traditional beliefs need some modification. When the holy books were being defined this possibility only interested a few; it was vigorously denied by others. The Pharisees believed that there would be a resurrection when the dead would reappear on this earth for judgement, but even this does not necessarily involve believing in a continuing life for man in some world other than this one.

Religion in the Old Testament is almost entirely concerned with this world and men and women living in it. Human life is within the control of God who creates it all and has a purpose in so doing. Within the complex of heaven and earth, land and sea, plants, fishes, reptiles, mammals, he includes man. God makes man like himself in so far as he is to be a controller and an organizer and have freedom of initiative. God has also endowed man with the capacity for communication with him and so for learning. Yet man's control is far from effective; his understanding of God's will is very imperfect; it seems that he is a slow learner. These limitations seem to be responsible for some, at any rate, of what is generally called 'evil'. Evil is enemy to God and enemy to man. Some believe that there are evil powers actively at work preventing man from making a fuller response to God.

In Israel's religion there is never any suggestion that such evil powers could succeed in the attempt to defeat God. The questions are How, When and Where will God choose to destroy the evil powers so that man's living can be established in a context in which God's creative purposes can be carried out? Whether in this world or elsewhere, God will decisively prevail. Hope stretches beyond the life-span of the believer and he realizes that he is looking forward to something he may never see. Some believe that the consummation will take place in another world, beyond time and space, a quite other context for the demonstration of God's power. Those who have been on God's side will enter on a new life and those who have been ranged against him will be destroyed. Some believe that the struggle is played out within the life-span of each individual and that for him death is the end; if the individual has been faithful and obedient God's will has prevailed and for him this is sufficient reward.

# 4

## WHAT THE OLD TESTAMENT IS
## ABOUT

The Old Testament is about the origins and growth of a great religion – great because it is still alive and powerful and because so many different peoples in many different times, including the present, have been inspired by it. It tells how one community in the ancient world established itself not by military conquest and political lordship but by developing an interpretation of human life and destiny which commanded respect and gained supremacy over the minds and hearts of many peoples. The strength of this position depends upon its positive and encouraging interpretation of human life: yet this is no easy-going optimism and indeed much of the Old Testament speaks of tragedy and doom.

The writers understand human life as having great possibilities and it is for this very reason that they interpret failure so severely and devote so much time to condemnation. This understanding of human living is set against an interpretation of the environment which is also positive and encouraging and contrasts strongly with interpretations which present it as largely hostile or merely neutral. In the Old Testament the environment is the living creation of a friendly supernatural power, not just an unalterable frame to be taken for granted as static and without significance of its own.

These understandings of man and the world belong to an interpretation of the whole *as* a whole. This whole is understood in this way because of the belief that it depends upon the will of one supreme God. Where it is supposed that man's life is controlled by many gods, powerful over different aspects of life and responsible for different peoples, there can be no underlying sense of unity or wholeness. But where it is believed that there is one supreme God, all aspects of life and all peoples come together within his dominion and theology becomes a theology of all that is. The conviction that this is so may be arrived at in two different ways: if there is but one creator God, man's life as such must surely be important; or, if man is convinced that his life is important, he may come to believe that it is lived in an environment created by one supreme God. In experience the two ideas grew side by side, reinforcing one another and flourishing because they are logically consistent. Being logically consistent does not make them true. It is equally consistent to say that the universe is self-existent and neutral and that man's living is likewise self-contained and neutral.

God as the Old Testament presents him is the maker and possessor of all things: without him nothing would exist at all. It is not possible to understand what the Old Testament is about without either believing this or entering in imagination into the lives of those who do. The great question remains as to whether the basic proposition is sound or not – very many doubt it. Almost by definition it can be neither proved nor disproved. But even if the basic proposition is sound it does not necessarily follow that everything in the Old Testament must be taken at its face value; there are enough contradictions in it to make this very difficult anyhow. So those of us who are deeply convinced about the basic proposition, as well as any who are willing to consider it as a possibility, have still to go on asking questions about the activity of God and the status of man. In so far as what the Old Testament says is true it is 'about God', but this does not mean that everything it says about God is true.

The Old Testament is also about man and his capacities and one of his capacities is that he can set values on things and make judgements about them. He can do this about what others have said about God and he *must* do this because it is his nature to test things and ideas for himself and only to accept authority when he is satisfied that the authority is securely based. No man's judgement is always right, and the fact of having reached a decision for oneself does not make it into a good decision, even though it may be right to act upon it until it turns out to have been mistaken. An athlete has to train and practise if he is to reach his best possible achievement; all human beings have to learn the exercise of good judgement by hard work and practice. In all this there are risks and many shrink from them.

God in the Old Testament is utterly to be trusted. It is assumed, for example, that sooner or later he will punish the wicked. He is expected to be entirely consistent and this is why he is so often expected to destroy, because what is not acceptable to him cannot survive. But equally he can be relied upon to preserve the integrity of man's sound judgements and to vindicate, not necessarily by the reward of material prosperity, the conduct of those who maintain the kind of living and thinking which is worthy of man made in God's own image. So the Old Testament is about faith, faith in two senses. It is about 'a faith' in the meaning of giving assent to certain statements of belief and it is about 'having faith' in a trust-worthy, faith-worthy God.

The basis of faith in God is not only his consistency but also his love and mercy. Because man is only man he can never completely fulfil his calling, he can never be entirely free of mistake, neglect and folly. But God's purposes would be totally frustrated if failure were always to cancel out everything else. God loves mankind, he nourishes man's growth and maturity as parents foster the health and welfare of children. Such human analogies are only partly useful for God's love is unfailing, he is merciful and forgiving and so again manifests his reliability and his strength. So the Old Testament is about love: about God's love for man and about man's calling to love God. Man's love for God is a devotion which is incomplete and uncertain; God's love for man is deep and unfailing.

Because God's love is deep and unfailing and his power great and inexhaustible there are great expectations and hopes, belief that the vision which Israel has glimpsed will shine clearly for her and for the whole world.

The LORD bless you and watch over you;
the LORD make his face shine upon you
   and be gracious to you;
the LORD look kindly on you and give you peace.

(Num. 6: 24–6)

# INDEX OF BIBLICAL REFERENCES

185

# GENERAL INDEX

Aaron 74
Abiathar 79
Abimelech 54, 56, 58, 78
Abraham 44, 118, 121, 122, 149
Absalom 80
Acco map p. 12; 15
Adam 119, 120
Adonai 115
Aelia Capitolina 66, 97
Ahab 55, 62, 81, 82, 144
Ahaz 82, 83
Ai map p. 32; 37, 43, 53, 75
Akhenaten 46, 74
Akkad, Akkadian 27
Aleppo 25; map p. 26
Alexander Balas 96
Alexander the Great 59, 63, 92, 93, 165, 166
Alexander Jannaeus 96
Alexandra 97
alphabet 48
Ammon, Ammonites maps pp. 12, 32; 21, 80
Amon 84
Amorites 43, 44, 60
Anatolia map p. 26; 29, 42, 45; see also Asia Minor
Anti-Lebanon mountains maps pp. 12, 26; 13, 17, 25
Antioch on the Orontes map p. 23; 93
Antiochus III, the Great 93, 94
Antiochus IV, Epiphanes 94, 169
apocalyptic 172, 173
Apocrypha 1, 2, 9, 101, 111, 112, 153, 171
Aqaba map p. 23; 13
Arabia maps pp. 23, 26; 11, 24, 45
Arabic language 36
Aram, Aramaeans map p. 12; 21, 62, 72
Aram Naharaim 29
Aramaic language 21, 36

Ark of God 143
Armenia map p. 26; 29, 97
Arnon, river map p. 12; 14
Artaxerxes I 90, 157
Artaxerxes II 90, 91, 157
Ashdod map p. 32; 22, 49, 77
Ashkelon map p. 32; 49, 50, 77
Asia Minor map p. 26; 25, 29, 45, 86, 93; languages spoken 21, 22
Asshur map p. 26; 27
Assyria, Assyrians map p. 26; 27, 61, 81-5
Aswan map p. 23; 24, 88
authority, of inherited ideas 9, 112, 148, 180; of scripture 102, 126, 128, 170

Baal 58, 68, 137, 144
Babylon, Babylonians map p. 26; 27, 84-7
Babylonian Chronicle 85
Bar Cochba (Simon bar Kosiba) 97
Barak 56
Bashan map p. 12; 19
Beersheba maps pp. 12, 32; 17
Behistun map p. 26; 87
Beth-shean (Beth-shan) map p. 32; 47, 49, 56
Beth-shemesh map p. 32; 48
Bethel map p. 32; 37, 53, 59, 144, 148
Bible, English 10, 115, 153; Greek 171, 172; Hebrew 1, 171, 172
Bronze Age 34, 35; Early 42, 43; Late 45-50, 54, 55; Middle 43-5, 49, 72
Byblos map p. 23; 47

Caesarea map p. 12; 15
Cambyses 87
Canaan, Canaanites map p. 32; 30, 43, 44, 47-51; Israelites settling 75-9, 123-5

187